THE SALT
BOOK OF
YOUNGER
POETS

Roddy Lumsden (born 1966) is a Scottish poet, who was born in St Andrews. He has published six collections of poetry, a number of chapbooks and a collection of trivia, as well as editing a generational anthology of British and Irish poets of the 1990s and 2000s, *Identity Parade*. He lives in London where he teaches for The Poetry School. He has done editing work on several prize-winning poetry collections and edited the Pilot series of chapbooks by poets under 30 for tall-lighthouse. He is organiser and host of the monthly reading series BroadCast in London. In 2010, he was appointed as Poetry Editor for Salt Publishing.

Eloise Stonborough was born in London in 1988. She studied English Literature at St Edmund Hall, Oxford where she won the Graham Midgley Prize for poetry and where she was also Secretary of the Oxford Poetry Society. She has recently completed a Master's degree in English, also at St Edmund Hall, and is beginning a DPhil at Balliol College, Oxford where she will be working on the connections between form and poetic personality in twentieth century poetry.

THE SALT BOOK OF YOUNGER POETS

Edited by

RODDY LUMSDEN

and

ELOISE STONBOROUGH

LONDON

PUBLISHED BY SALT PUBLISHING
Acre House, 11-15 William Road, London NW1 3ER United Kingdom

Printed in Great Britain by Clays Ltd, St Ives plc

Typeset in Monotype Joanna 10 / 13

ISBN 978 1 90773 10 5 paperback

1 3 5 7 9 8 6 4 2

CONTENTS

FOREWORD *by* Roddy Lumsden   xiii
INTRODUCTION *by* Eloise Stonborough   xv

RACHAEL ALLEN
    The Dolls   1
    Impotence   2
    from 4chan Poems   2
    Rag Bird   3
DAN BARROW
    An Inheritance   5
    2nd June 1916   6
    Edge   6
    from Even Ashes   7
JACK BELLOLI
    Yurt   9
    Loquation   10
    On Completing a Pocket Jigsaw of "The Fighting Temeraire"   11
JAY BERNARD
    Migration   13
    Tuesday Morning   15
    11.16   16
PENNY BOXALL
    Penny-farthing   18
    Navigavi   19
    Williams, Who Lived   21
    Taxidermy Outpost   22
JAMES BROOKES
    Opiates: Kaliningrad   23
    Hierophantic Head of Mao, Hunan Province   24
    In Clitheroe Keep I   24
    The English Sweats   25
PHIL BROWN
    South Bank   27
    Gamla Minnen   28
    Diptych   29
    Sir Gawain on the Northern Line   30

NIALL CAMPBELL

  After the Creel Fleet 32

  Bank Holiday 33

  The Tear in the Sack 34

  Hitching Lifts from Islanders 34

  The Apple 35

KAYO CHINGONYI

  Gnosis 36

  Fist of the North Star 37

  Guide to Proper Mixtape Assembly 38

  Some Bright Elegance 38

MIRANDA CICHY

  Bear 40

  Badminton 41

  Mackerel Sky 42

  The Grecian Widows 43

JOHN CLEGG

  Moss 44

  Kayaks 45

  Luz 45

  Antler 46

  Tribe 47

NIA DAVIES

  A History of the Ophicleide 48

  Transit Hours 49

  Harbour Bell 49

  Periphylla Periphylla 50

  Turning Edge 51

AMY DE'ATH

  Sonnet 53

  Poetry for Boys 54

INUA ELLAMS

  Of all the boys of Plateau Private School 59

  Portrait of Prometheus as a Basketball Player 61

  GuerrillaGardenWritingPoem 62

CHARLOTTE GEATER

  Moro 64

  Grotesquerie 65

  Not Goodbye 66

  Squalor 66

DAI GEORGE

New Translation 68

Plans with the Unmet Wife 69

Metropolis 71

Distraction During Evensong 71

TOM GILLIVER

The Graft 73

This Feather Stirs 74

Talking Back 75

Before We Thaw 75

EMILY HASLER

Cake Fork 76

Wet Season 77

The Cormorants 77

On reading the meaning of "falchion" in an encyclopaedia 79

OLI HAZZARD

Moving In 80

The Inability To Recall The Precise Word For Something 81

Arrival 82

Badlands 83

Prelude To Growth 84

DANIEL HITCHENS

Fruitbowl 85

First Shave After Coma 86

from Election 2010:

A Poetic Review 87

SARAH HOWE

A Painting 89

Faults Escaped 90

Crocodile 91

Chinoiserie 92

ANDREW JAMISON

The Bus from Belfast 94

The Starlings 95

Death's Door 95

Thinking About the Point of Things on a Spring Evening

on the Killyleagh Road 96

ANNIE KATCHINSKA

The Twenty Third Minute 99

Blue 100

Toni Braxton 101
February 102
ANDREW McMILLAN
from in my dreams you walk dripping from a sea journey
on the highway across America 103
Nabokov's butterflies 105
6:30am 106
obituary of a lesser East-European poet 106
SIOFRA McSHERRY
L'étoile 107
Faust 108
Sleepless 109
To a blackberry maggot 110
BEN MAIER
Gone Baby Gone 111
Gall 112
A Short History of Textiles 113
LAURA MARSH
The Winter Empress 115
Mistakes in Closed Captioning 116
Relics 116
The Wife's Lament 117
Apollo's Hyacinths 117
ANNABELLA MASSEY
A Gift of Lilies 119
Istanbul 120
Actress 121
JAMES MIDGLEY
Butterfly Antennae 124
Portrait of a Pig 126
The Invention of Faces 127
HARRIET MOORE
from Whalefall 128
Bog Bodies 131
The Ship of Theseus 133
HELEN MORT
Photography 134
Against Sleep 135
A Chaser for Miss Heath 138

CHARLOTTE NEWMAN

Dancing Prize 139

All That Jazz 140

Still Births 140

RICHARD O'BRIEN

Isthmus 144

Moses in Medieval Glass 146

Confessions of an Accidental Arsonist 146

RICHARD OSMOND

For the Nonce 148

Bait and Switch 149

Kunstkamera 150

Anatomist 151

VIDYAN RAVINTHIRAN

Ma 152

Jump-cuts 153

Recession 154

Dot Dot Dot 155

SOPHIE ROBINSON

Flesh Leggings 156

Winded By Love 157

Animal Hospital 157

from SHE! 158

CHARLOTTE RUNCIE

Staying In 160

The Seventh Winter 161

Pope, Telescope 162

Fur 162

In my pocket 163

ASHNA SARKAR

Heartbeat 165

Carry On Cutting 166

The New Vince 166

Setting Sun 167

WILLIAM SEARLE

Consider This 168

The Daimon 169

A Nocturnal Pact 170

A Visit 170

COLETTE SENSIER

Toothlessness 172

Orpheus 173

Evolution 175

WARSAN SHIRE

Ugly 177

Things we had lost in the summer 178

Maymuun's Mouth 179

Beauty 180

LAVINIA SINGER

The Mapmaker's Daughter 181

November 183

The Anchorite 183

Internal Memorandum 184

ADHAM SMART

The New Mechanics 186

Pumpkin Heart Boy 187

O, Openmouthed, You Are One of Us 187

MARTHA SPRACKLAND

Plate 189

Second Body 190

The Gold 191

Time Capsule 192

ELOISE STONBOROUGH

Fugue State 193

The Pharaoh's Embalmers 194

The Mercy Glass 195

Chaos 196

EMILY TESH

At Sea 197

(dona nobis pacem) 198

Three Sonnets for a Girl 198

JACK UNDERWOOD

And what do you do? 200

Under 201

My other girlfriends 201

Consequences 202

Certain 203

AHREN WARNER

Jardin du Luxembourg 204

Pictogramme   205
Engram   206
Avis   206
Epistle   207
BEN WILKINSON
First Glance   208
Filter   209
Sunday   210
The River Don   210
SOPHIE YEO
Love's Progress   211
Poem   212
Christmas, 1914   213
Nocturne   213

ACKNOWLEDGEMENTS   217

FOREWORD

by RODDY LUMSDEN

◇   ◇   ◇

After anthologising my own generation of poets in *Identity Parade* (Bloodaxe, 2010), I felt I wanted to bring together work by poets from a new generation of poets which promises to be a fruitful and varied one. It seemed important to find a co-editor from that generation so I asked Eloise Stonborough, on the understanding that I would insist on her inclusion in the anthology. When we drew up the list in autumn 2010, all the poets were aged 26 or under, born between late 1983 and 1992. Two fairly recent (and recommended) anthologies, *Voice Recognition: 21 Poets for the 21st Century* (Bloodaxe, ed. Byrne/Pollard) and *City State* (Penned in the Margins, ed. Chivers) featured poets from a younger generation but the editors set a higher age limit of mid 30s and I felt there were more than enough poets of great promise in the younger age band to warrant their own showcase.

We decided not to include poets who had published a full collection, though this ruled out only a handful of poets. We also decided not to set up an open submission process. These poets were selected from those who had already come to our notice (via magazines, readings, ezines, pamphlets etc) or who were recommended to us. We asked them to submit a body of work and, between us, chose what we felt were the strongest pieces. Already, since choosing the fifty poets here and gathering the poems, I have encountered more talented poets from this generation which promises to be a flourishing one.

INTRODUCTION

by ELOISE STONBOROUGH

◊ ◊ ◊

It isn't easy to "make it" as a poet today. At the time of writing, Arts Council funding cuts have put the futures of many small presses and magazines into question, and the already minuscule poetry lists of the major commercial publishers seem to be only getting shorter. And yet there is a vibrancy to the contemporary scene which comes directly from our younger poets. Young writers are not only getting involved with poetry in increasing numbers, contradicting its reputation as the purview of the middle-aged and middle-class, but they are making it their own: setting up new reading series, magazines, and workshops across the country. The Salt Book of Younger Poets is an attempt to capture some of that energy and make it visible to a wider audience.

This anthology presents the work of fifty poets aged 18–26, none of whom had published a full collection at the time of submission and several who have never published outside of student publications or online zines. While we are proud to have among our selection a number of poets who have already won the Eric Gregory, Foyle Young Poets and Tower prizes, or who have published pamphlets in the tall-lighthouse Pilot and Faber New Poets series; the names of many of the poets featured here will be unfamiliar even to diligent observers of contemporary poetry. Any anthology is designed both for those already familiar with a particular scene and for a general audience. This book, in particular, is intended to introduce new voices who are not yet ready for a collection of their own to readers—especially other young people—who may not be aware of the venues in which these poets are developing their work.

In asking only that our included poets were aged 26 or below we gave ourselves the freedom to select writers from across the poetic spectrum. We read poems which began as performances pieces alongside sonnets, avant-garde experiments as well as narrative lyrics. In a time when many poetry publications still struggle against tokenism, we believe that these poets are representative of the diversity of the contemporary poetry scene; proving, perhaps, the fallacy of the argument that selections based on merit will inevitably end up reproducing the status quo. There are, of course, trends to be found between these writers: a number of them are alumni of the major youth poetry competitions and creative writing courses; many were educated at Russell Group universities. While a conspiracy theorist will always find evidence of collusion, there is much to be celebrated in the fact that poetry is still attracting bright young minds.

Competitions such as the Foyle Young Poet and Tower Poetry Prizes have made becoming a poet seem possible for many young people, providing access to mentorship schemes and writing retreats that go a long way toward countering the isolation which dissuades many potential new talents. Similarly, the increasingly prevalent creative writing degrees offer a venue in which young poets can dedicate themselves to improving their craft under the supervision of more experienced writers. It has recently become commonplace to bemoan the institutionalisation of poetry, to claim that the inevitable result of workshopping is the "workshop poem". There is some truth in this fear. The example of the US shows how creative writing MAs can develop into a kind of academic Ponzi scheme: professional poet-teachers running courses devoted to producing the next generation of poet-teachers who have an economic incentive to reproduce the factional aesthetics and theoretical frameworks of their predecessors. What is less plausible, however, is that this problem will inevitably be replicated in the UK.

Courses and competitions are not the only route into poetry—nor should they be—but they are a remarkably effective method of introducing poets to one another. For young writers in particular, the communities created by these initiatives have drastically changed the routes into the field of contemporary poetry. This is, in part, the product of the new digital world in which anyone with a laptop and a free afternoon can set up their own magazine. But rather than privileging conformity, the publications and readings organised by these groups are new mode of poetic community: rejecting acrimonious factional divides and supporting a plurality of voices. Greater investment in developing young poets may well be British poetry's best chance to avoid a homogenous mainstream dominated by the aging figures of the old guard.

It is discomfiting, however, to have to reassess one's understanding of poetic allegiance. Already there are attempts to force these loose-knit groups into something approaching a traditional movement. A number of recent articles have dubbed them the "facebook generation" of poets for whom social networking and status updates matter far more than the craft of poetry. This is little more than patronising nonsense. While the internet may be providing young writers with access to like-minded peers, the quality of publications such as The Cadaverine, Cake Magazine, Clinic, Fuselit, Gists & Piths, Hand + Star, Pomegranate, and Stop Sharpening Your Knives (to name but a few) cannot be explained away by a facile reliance on the stereotypes of contemporary youth culture.

These clichés prevail because young writers have long been underrepresented in mainstream poetry. If the average age to publish a first collection is one's early thirties and one is a "young poet" until the age of forty, it is unsurprising that there is a widespread confusion between the "young" and the "new'. As the poets in this anthology show, age is not necessarily a requirement of experience. The poets in the following pages are young but they are not juvenile. Their poems are not adolescent outpourings nor precocious imitations of their literary heroes but rather the products of wide reading, hard work and talent. While their voices will, of course, continue to mature and develop, the poems included here are not merely placeholders of nascent promise but poems which can hold their own—and do—with the best work of their older contemporaries. One does not need to fetishize youth to see the importance of providing these poets with a space of their own: a chance for them to display their diversity of influence and interest as well as, we hope, revealing commonalities between poets from disparate poetic traditions.

There is an inherent contradiction between the role of the anthologist and that of the anthology. The anthologist is a collector; a magpie seeking out the brightest specimens of a particular moment. Anthologies are hampered, however, by their apparent definitiveness: their inclusions and oversights deciding who is "in" or "out" and often, when it comes down to it, who it is that *matters*. In naming this anthology *The Salt Book of Younger Poets* we have laid ourselves open to such charges of hubris as well as those—more damningly—of short-sightedness. Yet we do not pretend to have assembled a definitive catalogue of every younger poet. Instead, this book is intended merely to offer up a representative sample of the range of talented young voices in British poetry today. If the purpose of an anthology is, at heart, to recommend, then we hope this selection will raise the profile of fifty young poets whom we believe are worth watching as they continue to change the face of contemporary poetry.

THE SALT
BOOK OF
YOUNGER
POETS

RACHAEL ALLEN

◊ ◊ ◊

Rachael Allen was born in Cornwall in 1989. She studied English at Goldsmiths University and currently lives and works in London where she co-runs the poetry and art collective "Clinic Presents'.

THE DOLLS

An artichoke heart in a blood orange sprouts a stem,
growing fruit Babushka dolls, firm on stalks
up trellis, knocking in a warm allotment breeze.
You'll feed them in winter with a wife's wide smile
and harvest them, ripe in June. Breaking their polished
wood torsos from the root, until you reach the smallest bud,
the dense doll, her face the innards of a mottled tree.

There's a picture of my mother trussed in hospital wear
and in her arms a baby. Flowers and cards mean the bed's
a shop and there's a drip in her arm. I couldn't make it so far
— the rooting was easy to pass—I knocked the sac, sapling,
from a blood stem. It fell smooth as the wet necks of mallards.

I've raked the smallest of your gifts from my breasts.
Forgive me I never knew we were built for children.

IMPOTENCE

I thought it might be the waiter
bringing me the telephone as
they do in films to tell me my
mother had been hit by a bolt
of lightning or that war had
broken out and we needed to go.
How I prayed for this. It was the
waiter, opening up his grinning arms
to the erect pepper grinder, as large
as his leg, asking us "do you want
some?" You decline, I agree,
the grinder like the champing of teeth
on a wild sexed baboon.
In silence we wait for the final crunch.
I mention we should get one that big;
you nod. Glancing around, I chew
in questions, everyone around us has taken
everything to talk about, so that suddenly, after
years, we have nothing left to say.

from 4CHAN POEMS

/B/
(RANDOM)

Boxxy you are the home of the anonymous. I liked to read
on you all my false news it went across your head like The
Financial District and how you glowed with it. I got Tipp-Ex
and painted you as an angel on my childhood rucksack and
wore you proudly to school—you've got the kind of fame

of girls who killed other girls in childhood I wonder if you've ever seen lampposts in LA? Do they have crabs where you are? Sometimes everyone thinks you're dead. I saw a rainbow today but it had nothing on you. Your eyes held entire months of teenage summers when my skin smelt of a scented diary from the garden centre or an Impulse set from Safeways anyway I think where we lost you was somewhere in the Californian sun squint and glare.

/CM/
(CUTE/MALE)

When we play The Simpsons game where I find an episode of The Simpsons that is like real life I think about the presence of that squeeze of our shared childhood spent however many miles apart and I imagine us both rooted to a Sunday television with porcelain swans a baby gumming on a cork coaster with mottled animals on it aching bored afternoons spent grappling with our siblings — this was when our lives were never ending — gazing out of windows into suburbs where the pink dusk settles like a trapping net — maybe once our eyes met through a satellite or something I think maybe that's too romantic — how about you give me a picture of a verge of grass and a stream I'll show you there we are those tiny dots.

RAG BIRD

"During and after the Second World War the population boomed as a consequence of the Blitz. The bomb sites of the City provided an ideal habitat."

The birds became the seams, but looked un-seamed
like the thousands of rags created through war. De-peopled, unspined

the ghost clothes fly in to bank on the man-made screes
beneath the VASELINE advert, stuck on in a spirit white.

3

A spirit, white like the ones vicars thought passed up through churches.
Vicars who would hope, when reburying the already dead, blown feet away

from their graveyards, that these far-flung spirits would be able to find
their way back up through the damage

to where the birds watched everything. From their populous high place,
their aphrodisiac scree, they clothed the city with their non-stop breeding.

I heard for every building that lost a body, two birds moved in,
and some people said it looked like they were laughing.

DAN BARROW

◊ ◊ ◊

Daniel Barrow was born in Bournemouth in 1988. He studied English
Literature and Creative Writing at the University of Warwick, and is planning
to start postgraduate study in London in the autumn. He has poems in the
2010 *Tower Poetry* Summer School anthology.

AN INHERITANCE

Late night: my razor sprouts hair after one
sweep of the shoulder. Otherwise, these fronds
poke over my shirt line, then, scaling, join
my neck-forest. My father has the same
gorilla back. As heirlooms go, it's not
exactly bullion: another flaw
to make up Atlas' weight. On worst days,
to sweat in a jumper's better than stabbing,
wilting gazes, Lombroso's condemnation.

My father also gave me elsewhere: past
and place I'd have (with half a chance)
disowned; survival traits: breakfast habits,
his plaintless graft, his awful drain laughter.

And when tawdry life's novelty dissolves,
a back to go to: tunnels where the air
slows, gold and green; mud's feel, the thrushes' voice,
the smell of horse shit. Light and rain will speak
to earth: the rupture of an origin.

2ND JUNE 1916

After Franz Kafka

What a muddle I've been in with girls — in
spite of all my headaches, insomnia,
grey hair, defeat, I've verve enough left
to flourish eyes and flutter compliments.
Have spilled more ink, my ledgers tell me,
over the (at least) six since the summer
than on Frau F. Bauer — but then again,
she wants little to do with my pen.
All the city's flora: the trams,
the sweltering office typing pool, the square
where I traced their heelprints through snow, their furs
a burred flowering. The words trickle or
gush, but never cease to urge up, out —
to admire them, to proffer a hand until
admiration is bled out. One learns
almost to hate the world, so fine, so closed.

EDGE

David Bomberg, Evening, Cornwall, Towards St. Ives (1948)

And everything falls toward
the sea: the cliff's ruts, entropy of
the scumbled slips of late summer
crags cutting shade, aeon-deep split

from this onward spillage, shaded
like sandstone, alien hill slate.
Seeing double: my own brink
of afternoon, a year ago,
and this re-smeared memory. Cling
to artefacts—shards, words, mineral
language—they don't hold this warmth,
glister, the world's grip—the porous
solidity of bone. The swallows
from their cliff holes troubled sea air.
Am I right my to see my self
scanning this elided land, a point
of departure, notebook out.
Evening flickers, dissolves in strokes.
Lingering: one vast atlantic.

from **EVEN ASHES**

i.m Derek Jarman

II

When I was one, you *walked to the top*
of the Ness to watch a high sea under
a starlit sky. I only saw it
in photographs: the lunar scape of shingle,
a sea of tranquillity hewn into
salt-whiteness. Prospect, a tar-black tooth
set in the horizon
                    unfurling life
colour germinating on the negative.

When I was five, you were dead. It's only now
I'm catching up with your distant burning:
love is an anachronism, time buckled
by a fag at a boy's lips, a print of light,

7

days' sparks haunting the retina

                      Shine here

to us

    illuminate. Prelude to blue.

X

This living hand, now warm and capable
falls across the sheets — spent, again. The pricks
return each time with the morning bells.
My snakeskin strips off, your arm brushing mine.
The wishing ceased some time past — not for shame,
but knowing time's stone-scranching wear, the wrack
it leaves, of bone, of mottling burns

                      Thine own heart

dry of blood

       we were imprinted,
a trace on film, steadfast. Even ashes
will glow as they bleed, crumble, drift and rise
in points. The hearth, the air flits with poetry,
of no more speech than the whisper of reels.
Birthday.

       The may, the broom stay. Tell me how
they're growing.

      Fireworks.

        HB true love.

JACK BELLOLI

◊   ◊   ◊

Jack Belloli was born in London in 1990. He is currently studying English at Christ's College, Cambridge.

YURT

Last night, I learnt that "yurt" meant
the imprint made in the earth by a tent
before it came to mean the tent itself.

I pictured, at first, a hot semantic affair, a work of hands:
two surfaces pressed together, palm to palm,
printing meaning onto sheets of sand.
The soil bears the weight, and the tent in its turn takes the word

so that perhaps, for a moment, when pushed to their limits,
they meant each other, together.
The sheltered ground was boundless,
the earthed canvas not pegged down.

It's over now. The ground's a gasping hole.
Blown off, blown over. Tent got its tongue.

9

But, once myth folds, who really lies beneath?
What mixture of prophet and reckless historian
came upon those remains while coming over the dust?
How did he cross from vision to evidence,
to take in the print with the briefer Eureka of "Yurt!"?

And, why, at his word, did the tent rise—
not like a ghost but a hide-bound colossus,
solid yet involved in its hole, and ready to die?

I pictured the bending delegate of a race
old before its years and used
to living off such flotsam, on the scruff,
to reading in each shadow something toppling
to electing kings with one eye on their coffins
to seeing their ancestors only in the sandstorm.
Only they would be given to this post-Adamic brand
of names with a whiff of the damned.

Back there in the dark, I thought it wise
to define yourself by detritus,
to be named for the net result of all you'll do,

so I saluted you, Mr Two-Loving-Kids, Mrs Ten-Grand-in-Debt,
by switching on the light.

LOQUATION

It seems that hearing your words left me
in some ever-swelling toad's throat of a space,
untracked by syntax and with no inflection
beckoning like a flare. I struggle
even to draw blanks.

But, here, silence isn't signless.
As details in the walls start chattering,

the switches and planks are read
like buttocks or a babewyn's eye, admired
into glory only through the pause.

From this side of the glass and plaster,
lines which structure
are revealed as martyrs, witnessing
just in the way they buckle or
hang. It's in these minutes,

weighted like slowing snooker balls,
that each young sphere rolls out
till horridness gives way to constellation.
Something sure is founded in the ornaments
and seams themselves—so, now, I push
this pink and croaking zigzag into speech.

ON COMPLETING A POCKET JIGSAW OF "THE FIGHTING TEMERAIRE"

It starts and ends with frames.
The last and greater, with the strain against
its sides, lies in
the smaller first, not furled or coiled, slack
or deflated, not even waiting,
and barely unfulfilled

because the lens can still accept from here
the flare and rock-and-shadow—both atomic,
holding fire. Apart
from these, however, the eye's
rolled back to somewhere unenlightened, back
when telling sea from sky took art

enough. Still, one must
hold the line, must fan the crackle into its

slowly-rectangled
incense smoke—but the tide can't be held back.
The cobalt and reflection are themselves
leviathan and rise

before one's got around
to closing up the gap. The eye alights
on the minutest
click in a particle of dusk and watches it cluster. Strokes
submit to teeth, until crumbs sit
giddy, intact, somehow

unswallowed. At
the smacking of the split lips, all things turn in
for the night, towards their resting place. The recognition
of a certain yellow logic soothes. Indefinite
identities disappear
over each edge. Clouds groove,

scarcely arrested
at the border. The rigging, as had been ordained,
grasps the abyss here—and this
last chip of just off-centre essence is the only
conceivable end. We are far past
sheerness.

Whole, one
catches motion twice: first, in
that drawn-out half-romance of spray, sunset
and wetted knife, but then, in the less palatable fact
that piece is fighting volatile
piece, all ready to break.

JAY BERNARD

◊ ◊ ◊

Jay Bernard was born in 1988 and is from London. She studied English Literature at Oriel College, Oxford and is currently living in London. Her first pamphlet was *Your Sign is Cuckoo, Girl* (tall-lighthouse) followed by appearances in the anthologies *City State* and *Voice Recognition*. She is 2011 / 2012 poet in residence for the National University of Singapore.

MIGRATION

There have been so many last days.
So many fill this earth, their eyes rolled
backwards, their lungs deflated.
The translucence that hangs between
dusk and twilight, dawn and high noon
is coloured navy and it is that blue
of stagnant blood beneath the skin,
that blue of clouded eyes and dried tongues,
that blue of migration that I recognised
in the wastes of this evening.

I rode from Balham to Charing Cross.
The tunnels were arterial,

the intermittent lamps like a spinal constellation
and each station was a throbbing heart,
as close and as far as you are from the world
when asleep in the dark of your father,
passing from one phase of silence to another,
swimming through the low light, the dim glow
cast by a thin skin, that despite its love of life
will never last.

Primrose Hill is filled with skeletons.
Walk alone in the late afternoon
and you'll see the blossom is the colour of bone;
the gale that picks up around midnight
is the collective force of all of us speaking
as we sleep; and the March breeze in your lover's
hair is the remnant breath of those who died mid-speech.
These guttural sobs punctuate the story
of the city, the only story that's ever been told:
the swift decline of transient glory.

The street is quiet when I leave the station.
The thin curtain of today has been drawn,
but I can see tomorrow through the gap:
tomorrow the road will be clotted with cars,
mats rolled out and knees bent in prayer;
someone will miss their stop, someone will be deported,
someone will die in their chair. The translucent sheet
that hangs between eras will still be the colour
of the strange mist on a plum, heavy and simultaneously
light, sweet, cold, perceived with tearful gratitude
and aching regret; star blue, cyan blue,
the far azure of Pluto —

if you're the last person to leave, please turn out
the lights and be in the next great city by morning.
If darkness catches you and you turn back to see
the blank menace of so many windows,
imagine the fear of the first people huddled, haunted
one hundred, thousand years ago.

TUESDAY MORNING

I wake earlier than usual,
   startled suddenly from dreamless sleep.
     One eye opens. Crook neck. Wet cheek.

Damp sheets tangled round my feet.
   Except, I do not turn and stretch, yawn,
     as when I wake into full dawn —

air-blue, crystal June mornings
   when the room is webbed as though
     I'd slept in a milk-grey fog now rising;

I do not move, but something ebbs —
   some small internal me wants to stretch
     to their full height. They detach themselves,

unpeeling their skin from my inner limbs.
   In the dark morning, lit with red stars
     and Venus setting, they turn, they climb,

they wedge a foot in the groove of my groin
   then vanish. They leave, gone, enjoined
     with a cargo of my thoughts, all my lies, my lungs,

my regrets, my unadmitted wrongs; I'm left
   hollow in the bed. Light strung-out with lamplight
     trickles in. Whoever they were, they've gone.

Whoever was here, whatever woman lay
   down to sleep last night has alighted from
     the train of blood, of fat and all that relates

to the plight of someone who never stopped
   to see what inward sign was blazing;
     how our design is such that our bodies absorb

the most immaterial of things,
  and as host to racing thoughts, prone
    to idiocy and loss, I get up, dress, and disregard

that how I want to feel is never how I feel.
  People stare in the street. Touch is obsolete,
    reflection gone. I cannot feel my fingers or my feet.

No thought moves me except that this is what I need.

11.16

Sometimes, I'm caught short at the station whilst waiting
for the 11.16; sometimes, I see its tiny grey lights on the horizon,
and with crossed legs and an urgent bowel, I think, I think, I think
I'd better go.

I push open the heavy doors in to a lav whose decor takes something
from the wet room at Abu Ghraib. The first cubicle houses a smashed
cistern where some woman finally lost it—but the drunk, blind, desperate
have continued to use it anyway.

The second cubicle has fag burns on the seat. Since childhood, when my
eyes were level with that plastic ring, I have hated those long, brown stains
that look so much like shit it distresses me. How often I've hovered
above them, gripping the paper holder . . .

But I am always surprised at the third—the third at the far end
with writing across the walls. Some letters are large as ads,
some an illegible signature, some an illegible scrawl—
someone has drawn a woman without a head,

or breasts. Just black blood in black biro spilling on the numbers
of models or pimps or pretenders: call 86754421 for HOT THAI;
Call 73340796 for FUN TIME. And sequestered in the corner,
a rhyme from a fellow poet:

They fuck you up the government
You may not know it but they see
That you're a mug and so you'll spend
Nine grand on what they got for free

On cold, December mornings when you're squatting in a council loo,
it's a warming thought to think that women before you have thought
to rummage for a pen, and write the things they think: "Good luck!"
says one, "It's a scam!" says two, "Fight back," says three,

"Shut up," says four, "You whining Marxist pig. You fat mother-
fucker, you stupid whore. You dick. Fuck you, you twat."
Such things offer up their own reward. The poet returned
and in the scribble, the mess, the scrawls:

Perhaps (she wrote)
You're lucky that you can hate my poems
And never be haunted by the ghosts

That compel me to write them —
Those figures of history
Who whisper "do something."

PENNY BOXALL

◊　◊　◊

Penny Boxall was born in Surrey and grew up in rural Scotland and Yorkshire. She graduated in 2009 from UEA where she completed an MA in Creative Writing (Poetry). Her poetry has appeared in *The Rialto*. In 2009 she was the Literature intern at The Wordsworth Trust. She now works at the Ashmolean Museum.

PENNY-FARTHING

Perched like a bird on a spun nest,
this is how to soar while sitting still.
You sense speed rather than feel
it: the crowd slipping as though
it was no big thing; the trees hanging
on and the iron rails zipping
in vertical flashes.
            This is what it is
to be on top: both the giant
and needy Jack, high on his own
sprung apparatus. Spin past
the tilted hats in a blur
of concentrics—like the spread

of a raindrop in water, this is a trick
of near-misses.
      Dismounting's another:
such pomp calls for an end
on a grand scale. Slide,
wobbling, to the zoo; befriend
a giraffe. Eat peanuts
by the monkey cage. Feel
how the firm ground shifts
with each footstep. The big
machine is chained to the gates,
useless without your slim propulsion;
      though it is something to be god,
high and probably, therefore, mighty,
the world a wheel of secret orbits
whirring below and never touching.

NAVIGAVI

They sent my father's father to the desert.
He worked on aeroplanes and tanks,
a seed inside their boiling metal husks.
He tickled the wheeze of purpose
from the scrap while the world spun
with propellers.
      At night, he lay on
the cold sand and by day he stood
on the hot sand.
      Once, a beetle,
seeing no other way, blundered
into his ear. It swam the tiny orbit
of his hammer and anvil, a waxy
navigation, and was amber-trapped
before either of them knew it.
      It had genesis
in the hot human cave of an ear.
It bent to my grandfather's work

as he did, heard the bombers
guzzling like bees.
     When they sent for him,
he carried it aboard, a tiny cargo.
In the canal of his ear
it kept its own horizon
while the sea brought his stomach
aching to his mouth.

Unknown, it was the mascot
of the man for years. He carried it
through the rain and it heard things meant
for him.
     It buzzed with his vow,
trembled in response; and buried
the keenness of my father's
baby cry—if he slept on the good ear
he was untroubled.
     Strange, then, that he allowed
castor oil into his head.
It slipped past the hard stone
which someone whipped out
with a cotton bud.
     The new noise,
that first unhindered day,
was dumbfounding.
He couldn't miss a thing.
     But he kept the beetle—
if that is the word for
the rattling nut
hooked from his head—
in a jar. If you asked it, it would
say, *I have sailed.*

WILLIAMS, WHO LIVED

When this man was hauled from the foam
and, shaking, asked his name, the news spread fast.
They skimmed him back to shore —
a talisman, breaking the waves like eggs.

Hugh Williams had lived before. The name
confounded shipwrecks, made men float
through salted depths towards the aching
light. Williams was a lonely but a living sort.

It seemed the surest way to last gulp air not water,
to die dry, was to be him, or if not him
another of his kind. The parish registrars
scrawled Williams upon Williams as if they kept

forgetting. Williams married Susan, married
Mary, married Anne; and when he died,
(and died — and died —) the headstones
read the same, like yesterday's paper.

Williams stayed at home and picked rocks
from the binary of ploughed earth.
Or travelled, wrote a book; did/
did not like onions; wet the bed.

And when he went to sea — as captain,
passenger, stowaway — he kept himself
to himself: threw the name around him,
vein-strung, tenuous as a caul.

Note: Three men — each named Hugh Williams — were the sole survivors of three separate shipwrecks in the 17th, 18th and 19th centuries.

TAXIDERMY OUTPOST

We drive past the sign at first,
swerve, spin back.
                        It's hung
with skin, the crown of some
wrecked animal topping it all.
                They sell scented candles
and the recent dead —
a baby bear sits on a stool
                as if for a lesson,
his giant paw missing nothing
but a crayon.
                There's a pornographic hush
towards the back, the pelts
strung in moneyed lines,
shining like polished wood.
Leopards maul the walls.
                And a faun/not faun,
hauled from its mother,
is frozen in a pose it never struck,
its eyes filmy.
                        Outside is the Wild
which we only know about
because we know too of outposts
filled with fur. And look:
                here is a chipmunk
paddling a canoe, his little fist
just like yours.

JAMES BROOKES

◊   ◊   ◊

James Brookes was born in 1986 and grew up in rural Sussex. He read English and Creative Writing at the University of Warwick and then studied at the College of Law, Guildford. He is currently the Williams Librarian at Cranleigh School in Surrey where he also teaches English and History. In 2009 he received an Eric Gregory Award from the Society of Authors; his pamphlet *The English Sweats* was published by Pighog Press in the same year. He was awarded a Hawthornden Fellowship in 2011. His first full collection is forthcoming from Salt in 2012.

OPIATES: KALININGRAD

Scilicet the bar at the back of the restaurant:
ampoules of creosote, methadone, spermaceti.

You have in your possession
the medal for the capture of Königsburg:

a brimstone of cupro-nickel, saffron of tarnish.
Agreed. You may have passage

to the lost Amber Room. Where fire
burnished the quarters, the Löbenicht and Kneiphof,

to a shell case brass, there's now a nuclear
installation; a cartel of tonic peddlers.

By knocking off time, the sun is in suspension,
joyless at its weight as alloyed gold.

HIEROPHANTIC HEAD OF MAO, HUNAN PROVINCE

Whether he ever had the sweeping hair
of Keats or Shelley, is not for us to say.
Nor is there injustice in the air
of meditation, or the quiet way
his gaze is fixed, refuses to relent.
Perhaps the smooth-lipped stone looks indigent
above the lush and level park. Perhaps so,
but the mouth, which neither beams nor sneers
recalls a man who's just shut up. We know
culture is height; that's how it should appear
at pedestal level. Far above here
the terse sun will reach, then pass its zenith
content in power's more pedantic truth:
culture is length of shadow.

IN CLITHEROE KEEP I

The point was still to hold the pass, control
the pack-horses' route over the Pennines

—thus, Clitheroe. Up on its hill-spur. Small
infringement, herald of a bad time

like the taxman's strongbox on arrival
slung above the stirrups, half a wind chime.

a bright wind, marching east for Pendle hill;
a sinew below its heather-coat of mail.

Clitheroe. A rest home, heroes in choky,
the climate and recline of locked-up kings

bookmarked as if bored by their own stories.
Clitheroe in air, spring's chilblain kind

or callous devils, cast in the scitter-tourney
or called time hourly to its witching song

a bright wind-marching, east for Pendle hill;
a sinew below its heather-coat of mail

the slick hauberk of rain and a Lancs postcode
the box of weather, a clear fill and reload

barely keepsake by the re-pointing of stones
by wind, by everything else that's just coming, just gone.

THE ENGLISH SWEATS

Laid out in the field
is a Doomsday town
depopulated by *sudor anglicus.*

And up on the hill
past the rectory
the heir looks up his marriage in Debrett's:

the year that he learnt
the bark of muntjac
mating or birthing from the scream of a child;

to tell the marquee
and the caterers' van
from the unmarked car and the white tent rising.

Sometimes in his dreams
his father's spirit
caught by the creeping terror of the "new build",

shows him a pistol
kept in the desk drawer
to plug his Château Pétrus with dumdum rounds

or his grandfather
still coming for him
on a transport ship from the pas-de-Calais,

wrists bound saltire-wise
to the ensign pole,
ankles drumming their tattoo on the transom.

PHIL BROWN

◊　◊　◊

Phil Brown was born in Surrey in 1987. He attended the University of Warwick in 2005 and now works as a secondary school English teacher at Greenshaw High School in Sutton. In 2009 he was shortlisted for the Crashaw Prize and won the Eric Gregory Award in 2010. He has had his work included in *Dove Release: New Flights and Voices* (Worple Press, ed. David Morley), Dr. Rhian Williams' *The Poetry Toolkit* (2009, Continuum) and his debut collection is due for release with Nine Arches in 2012. He is the Poetry Editor for the online magazine and chapbook publisher, Silkworms Ink.

SOUTH BANK

Smoking in front of the Royal Festival Hall
adoring how strange we all are
on our private routes to
oh, just about everywhere there is to go.

The man with the thick black moustache
that intercepts some of his coffee,
the lady with dark purple lipstick
who does not look much like a lady,
the unslept man with his beautiful

greasy long hair who pokes
at his physics textbook whilst shivering
at the snidey breeze of the Thames,

young girls still hugging their new selves
made fresh for university with their proud
berets, and me hoping that someone
at this moment is finding me weird

for something I am doing or wearing.
Weird creatures of London, thank you
for your efforts, I love you all.
I love you all, London eccentrics, I love you all.

GAMLA MINNEN

after Wallace Stevens

so
I sit
at this
untuned piano
in Practice Room #5,
where the sound of off-key opera
and botched scales leak in from the surrounding walls,

missing you.

I
resurrect you
in the corner clumsily
clutching at notes as we sing
landlocked blues while the skylight
dims and you flick on the fluorescent bulbs
and somewhere a bus turns up late to an empty

stop.

A
kid
spills water
on his laptop. A feeble
roar spills from a malcontent lion
in some melancholy zoo. A crisp packet blows
defiantly out of a bin and we're just singing until our throats

dry out.

I
consider
the freezethaw effect
when fingering your name into
the cold window vapour or sipping the
marshmallows from your *chocolat chaud*. Funny though
now, to pass on pavements, reset as strangers glazed with facades as
   though ignoring

each other for the first time.

DIPTYCH

ACROSS

2. Campus in a wasteland (10)
6. A town hid in for a weekend (10)
7. Paper I scour for horoscopes (5)
9. A meal blackened in an oven (5)
11. The girl living in the floor above (4)
12. A disapproving brother (6)
14. Old ballroom in the midlands (3,3,5)
15. A train station I avoid now (6)
18. A book filled with photos of cats (1,3,3,13)
19. The girls' school that broke you (10)

1. A dessert we shared (5,6)
3. The end of the Piccadilly Line (8)
4. The town that took you back (5)
5. The boy who waited there for you (5)
8. A poem written on a postcard (3,3)
10. A restaurant in an airport (4,5)
13. A number on a door (8)
14. A song you sing better than the original (4,3)
17. A form filled in when the trouble started (5,3,7)
20. Something unsolvable (2)

SIR GAWAIN ON THE NORTHERN LINE

"In god fayth," quoth the goode knight, "Gawan I hatte,
That bede the this buffet, quat-so bifalles after,
And at this tyme twelmonyth take at the another
Wyth what weppen so thou wylt, and with no wyy elles
on lyve."

and if fate should fling me onto
the electric rail of a tube's tracks
to be sliced open with steel wheels
let me stay so mangled as to remain
unidentifiable and let the driver lose
no sleep.

Or if my end should be the slow sort
made more moral
with each cigarette I suck to the tip
allow me the time to close my accounts
and make good on old
promises.

Let death deal me the bravery to apologise
for piquant truths and pretty lies
and let my last words yield
more answers than questions
and the humility to acquiesce to
                    all suggestions.

Let my obituary eat up no more column
inches than those not born into old money
and should I be murdered at alighting
in Burnt Oak amid the fourth concentric
Zone let the artist of my death
                    escape.

The terms, though not of my choice, were agreed
and as I course viral underneath this metropolis
I leave my regrets at Embankment, Euston, Camden Town
like a skin shed, baring my raw jelly.
No more words sir, my naked neck is
                    rightly yours.
          The night deliquesces us all
          under the looming street lamp necks
          to be human altricial
          in the city's warp and weft.

NIALL CAMPBELL

◊ ◊ ◊

Niall Campbell was born on South Uist, the Western Isles of Scotland, in 1984. He studied English Literature at Glasgow University, and then took a Creative Writing MLitt at St Andrews University. In 2011 he was awarded a Robert Louis Stevenson Fellowship and an Eric Gregory Award. He currently lives in Glasgow.

AFTER THE CREEL FLEET

I never knew old rope could rust, could copper
in its retirement as a nest for rats.

The frayed lengths knotting into ampersands
tell of this night, and this night, and this,

spent taut between the surface and the sea floor —
the water coarsening each coiled blue fibre:

and, strained, one strand might snap, unleash its store
of ripples to be squandered in the dark,

yet thousands would remain still intertwined,
and thousands do remain, though frailer now.

These hoards, attached to nothing, not seen since
the last tightrope was walked, the last man hung.

BANK HOLIDAY

Today, the *is* is at ease with what isn't.
The local trains not running, the wood of

the sleepers lie a trampled orchard in a line,
who's pale ghost-fruit now ripens on the track.

Unoccupied, we can choose what dream to open:
childhood, or expectations, or that often

raised lid of being somewhere else.
I sleep on my back in a foreign town

where the birds are blue and long-winged,
and folk are gifted in the arts of welcome,

greeting everything they touch and stretching out
to welcome first the midday, then the evening sky.

I'll stay all day here in this company,
then leave for home by the longest route

afforded to the daydream, and repossess
the days I make do with, the unstamped letters,

reminders of things I don't forget;
the ghost-fruit lying mouldered on the track.

THE TEAR IN THE SACK

A nocturnal bird, say a nightjar,
cocking its head in the silence
of a few deflowering trees,
witnesses more than we do
the parallels.
                    Its twin perspective:
seeing with one eye the sack-
grain spilt on the roadway dirt,
and with the other, the scattered stars,
their chance positioning in the dark.

HITCHING LIFTS FROM ISLANDERS

A few turns in and conversation was strained.
We talked in fits about the boat crossing,
if only because it was one thing we shared,
as if some lost, great aunt. Then sport, then nothing.

Though there was that hour past Kilfinnan
we spent unspooling images of home:
the views from our parents' houses; the flares,
"their lit hearts", falling over Uist at New Years.

But one of us remembered too quickly
our home-taught reticence, regretted
having said too much, or too openly.
The next forty miles were the radio's.

Then we passed Buachaille Etive Mor,
its bracken and firs sprouting off the rock.
"That's one fucker of a fucker, eh?" he said.
"Aye, man, you took the words right out of my mouth."

THE APPLE

I grew suspicious when it didn't rot,
still red as the day it was given, possessed
with that enduring *slap* when caught, just right.

Secretly though, I began to weight it
sure that if it was wax the few lost grams
of seeds and stones, would tell in the palm.

But they didn't. And I could never risk a bite
so threading a thin wick into the flesh
like its own white worm, I flared a match—

only I didn't, and I won't. I'll spark
no light. I'll take the darkness, and the doubt.

KAYO CHINGONYI

◊ ◊ ◊

Kayo Chingonyi was born in Zambia in 1987 and came to the UK in 1993. He studied English Literature at The University of Sheffield where he co-founded a poetry night called "Word Life'. His poems are published in *City Lighthouse* (tall-lighthouse, 2009), *The Shuffle Anthology* (Shuffle Press, 2009), *Verbalized* (British Council, 2010), *Paradise by Night* (Booth-Clibborn Editions, 2010) and *The Best British Poetry 2011* (Salt Publishing, 2011). He is a visiting writer at Kingston University.

GNOSIS

"It is possible for you to reach it but you will grieve a great deal" — *The Gospel of Judas*

Imagine the husk of a man who knows
his son will die before the week is out.
You ask him why he sings, no doubt, baffled
by the faith it takes to open the most
stubborn of hearts, make a bloom of gently
insistent beauty. This is when your own
newly sprung bloom would shut itself again;
afraid that get well cards are only empty

measures of sentiment, the weight of a word.
You're sorry with no answer to this obscene
riddle: a stubble headed boy whose scream
fissures the night ward watched by a just lord
who won't intervene, for all this man stops
to find the tune that, even now, isn't lost.

FIST OF THE NORTH STAR

A pound and I'm the man
with seven scars, true heir
to the school of Hokuto

Shinken, wandering the non-
descript badlands that always
mean world's end, lone hero,

the criminally insane mutated
to pale hulks, their bulbous heads
made flesh-bombs with the flick

of a wrist so quick it seems
I only stand still, win by an act
of will. This is a Hokuto master's

art: observe the foe's stopped heart,
intact, but for the dark spot where
the strike found its mark. I practised

first with melons. When they split
at the slightest touch, I called myself
a novice. When we cut them open

to see the fruit reduced to slush,
I became a student. When my finger-
tips moved as if full metal jackets,

I set off on the quest that is my life's
work. Chain-wielding bikers cannot
faze me. To face me is to invite death.

GUIDE TO PROPER MIXTAPE ASSEMBLY

The silence between songs can't be modulated by anything other than held breath. You have to sit and wait, time the release of the pause button to the last tenth of a second so that the gap between each track is a smooth purr, a TDK or Memorex your masterwork. Don't talk to me about your mp3 player, how, given the limitless choice, you hardly ever listen to one song for more than two minutes at a time. Do you know about stealing double As from the TV remote so you can listen to last night's clandestine effort on the walk to school? You say you love music. Have you suffered the loss of a cassette so gnarled by a tape deck's teeth it refuses to play the beat you've come to recognise by sound and not name? Have you carried that theme in your head these years in the faint hope you might know it when it finds you, in a far-flung café, as you stand to pay, frozen, and the barista has to ask if you're okay?

SOME BRIGHT ELEGANCE

"and all his words ran out of it: that there
was some bright elegance the sad meat
of the body made" — "The Dance", Amiri Baraka

For the screwfaced in good shoes that paper
the walls of dance halls, I have little patience.
I say dance, not to be seen but free, your feet
are made for better things. Feel the bitterness
in you lift as it did for a six year old Bojangles
tapping a living out of Richmond beer gardens

38

to the delight of a crowd that wasn't lynching
today but laughing at the quickness of the kid.

Throw yourself into the thick, emerging pure
reduced to flesh and bone, nerve and sinew.
Your folded arms understand music. Channel
a packed Savoy Ballroom and slide across
the dusty floor as your zoot-suited twenties
self, the feather in your hat from an Ostrich,
the swagger in your step from the ochre dust
of a West African village. Dance for the times

you've been stalked by store detectives
for a lady on a bus, for the look of disgust
on the face of a boy too young to understand
why he hates but only that he must. Dance
for Sammy, dead and penniless, and for the
thousands still scraping a buck as street corner
hoofers who, though they dance for their food,
move as if it is only them and the drums, talking.

MIRANDA CICHY

◊   ◊   ◊

Miranda Cichy was born in London in 1988 but grew up in Bedfordshire. She studied English Literature at the University of Cambridge where she jointly won the Brewer Hall Prize for poetry. She was shortlisted for an Eric Gregory Award in 2010 and currently lives and works in London.

BEAR

We met in civilisation; someone had dressed you
in a suit. Brown hair rustled taut beneath the shirt
and nudged over the collar, I dropped my eyes
as the bear books said I should. Later I walked
to the centre of the woods to find you,

bare, clothes shed beneath the tallest tree.
Some suggest lying on the ground, and passively
waiting for the bear to lose interest. The earth
was fleshy soft, the leaves like damp confetti
as your claws trailed ragged across my back.

In the morning I passed bees like cherries
through your swollen lips, purring black and yellow

lamentations as their tiny bones cracked.
But *bears generally lead solitary lives*. I backed
away with my palms up, speaking calmly.

I saw you dance just once, with lumbering steps,
circling the keeper whose hands mauled your fur,
the chains looped round your paw and hers.

BADMINTON

That summer you strung a net between us
and lobbed a shuttlecock, a word that moulted
feathers in its wake. Back and forth

we stretched and hurled, overhead and underarm,
nudged those shots that gently tipped the net
or threw our force and slipped through air.

We heard the apples drop, the conkers crack,
but kept the patch trim with our feet,
stomping a court while grass grew tall

and walled around us. The days got cold,
the nights got darker, distant buses
overtook the chimes of ice cream vans,

you skidded on your knees to catch one low
and found the ground was hard as bark,
your shirt was boarded up with sweat,

the birds were long since dead within their trees.
Walking me home, the strings slapped slack
against our thighs. All night I dreamt of rain,

the way the court was pelted, melted
into mud, a bog with sinkholes
where we'd served or stood. And if I strained

I heard the sodden cracks each time
your racket tried a shot, and then the silence
where I should have answered back.

MACKEREL SKY

This portends thunder, you say, maybe snow.
In the streets the women spread their nets

and wait, slit eyed under headscarves, ready
for what was called a one-man miracle

on a mountain years ago. You lick the air
and spit out grains of salt, watching

the clouds begin to writhe their tails
and the sun sink like a small head under water.

When it falls we're halfway home, the first
slapping my shoulder, a large one

fat with its cat's tongue rub of scales,
jumping down my back to pavement

that's filling with slates of grey,
rolling with eyes. We must be quick, I say

bruised wet by each weight, mouths gulping
at our ankles. You stop and crouch

close to the ground, press your palm
on a head whose tail flaps at your sleeve,

the sky draining, your mouth flat, the air sharp
with the tang of something human and internal,

and watch me watching you, like a fish
watches the hook that draws it up.

THE GRECIAN WIDOWS

They have been born like this: in black,
fat-cheeked, with rolling pin arms
and tight, watchful eyes. They plant themselves

on stools along the hilltops, a squat of crows
who know that we'll approach them from below—
that we will stagger up knees crooked,

that the heat will make our faces slack.
They nod to see us place our palms
across the sun to see them, a salute.

They let their daughters smile back—
those crops of tired women wearing blue,
rubbing shoulders or their mothers' feet.

Their husbands build the hotels in the town,
men who smoke and spit and crease and dig
their heart diseases all day long, brown men,

men dirty white with dust, like bone.
The widows wash their daughters' frocks
with hard soap, as if for the last time.

JOHN CLEGG

◊　◊　◊

John Clegg was born in 1986 and grew up in Cambridge. He lives in Durham, where he is studying for a PhD on the Eastern European influence in contemporary poetry. A full collection is forthcoming from Salt in 2012.

MOSS

We feared the moss. We hollowed out
our ancestors and packed them with it,
left them smouldering in bark canoes.
On terminal moraines we blessed the moss
as herald of the thaw. Our children
got down on their knees to kiss it.
Kind moss insulated our pagodas,
bedlinened the herder on high pasture,
kindled grubby smoke for sacred visions.
We combed the moss. Our mosseries
were envied by the Emperor himself.
Spore cases, every size and colour, hung
like fireworks. We bred moss patiently,
too subtle work for human lifespans.
In the war we mulched the telegrams

demanding anaesthetic or poison moss.
Our holy valley stayed unoccupied.
Today, the only sound above a whisper
is the meal gong. I meditate at night
on whether we are really growing moss.
Our mystics say the moss is growing us.

KAYAKS

Our uncle in prison
sculpts bearpelts from soapstone,
tattooed his own shoulder:
a road gang of caribou

gnawing the tundra,
the musk ox, the grey goose,
my brother and I
racing kayaks on meltwater.

LUZ

Another body brought to me. I root
red-handed through the lights and cooling meat

and every bone I dredge I plunge in brine
as if it was a paintbrush. Flexing fine-

tipped jeweller's pliers in the corpse
I snag the earbones, hammer, anvil, stirrups,

each smaller than my smallest fingernail.
The bone I'm looking for is smaller still.

No pounder crushes it, no earthly fire
raises down its length one hint of char.

Leave it to marinate in fluoric acid
and it won't dissolve. Joachim Hachasid

claims it as the last bone in the spine.
Vesalius labels this the *Juden Knöchlein*:

jew-bone or resurrection bone or *luz*,
the almond out of which the body grows

again on Judgement Day. I scour and scour
for the tiny seed, the tight-packed flower.

ANTLER

An odd claw of bone
from the hub of the head,
once covered in velvet
and cabled with blood

now ossified utterly —
only the swerve
and feint of its grip
like a magnified nerve

to mark it organic.
It twists like a thought —
a petrified thicket
which broke in the rut.

TRIBE

They turn the lamb with a fan belt
that runs from the spit to the drum
of a stripped-down washing machine.
They pick their teeth with skink ribs
and sleep in the wrecks of taxis.
Most physical contact is eschewed
except in breeding season. Even then
their courtships are uncomfortable
and surly. Children are born albino.
Twins, since they fuse in the womb,
without exception kill the mother.
Shamen and doctors are frowned upon.
The headman and his closest allies
host mock dinner-parties in the wreckage.
Their small-talk—as far as we can tell—
is ritualised and meaningless to all.
Since there's no love, there's also
not much war. The major killer's boredom.
Our only photographs are from above.

NIA DAVIES

◊　◊　◊

Nia Davies was born in Sheffield in 1984. She studied English at the University of Sussex where she won the first Stanmer Prize for poetry. In 2008 she was awarded a place on the Academi Mentoring Scheme for Writers to develop her first novel *Polaris*. She works for Wales Literature Exchange and Literature Across Frontiers — a European platform for literary translation and intercultural dialogue. She has lived in Wales and is currently based in London.

A HISTORY OF THE OPHICLEIDE

> Eclipsed by tuba and euphonium
> and their careful marketing plans,
> I was a half-buffed shoulder pipe.
> A thorny funnel coiled over biscuit-dry
> jumpers. I had thunder-rushing arms.
>
> When you parped me you had to lean out-jointed,
> asymmetrical. I was already obsolete.
> But some hung onto me, hooked
> their brassy passion around my U-bend or
> atticboxed me in their instrument archives.

I was forced early into retirement but for rare
nights when I was air glossed with
breathy spit and I picketed to be kept live.
But my throb fell flat in the pond of other pipes,
their other useful selves ascending.

TRANSIT HOURS

Each day, when you button up your daily rucksacked armoury
and pull your knees out from under their morning swivels,
you become rinsed and flat packed,
ready to dismantle timber framed vows to yourself
and take a tied down barrow full of score
to work on you back. You pace through, unmellow,
your shoelaces tousled out, your toe knuckles raw.

You'll drag on behind a shadow plough,
with a hand in this, a cheek on that,
marry the cool brow to the fighting jaw,
snag yourself sore on occasional crosshatched junctions,
your weapon of choice a cup of hot flavoured milk.
On every important hour you'll scrape, clamour
or yawn for an exit, for the door.

HARBOUR BELL

All night, the wind on the high water mark,
coming in patterings and tired rushes.
The buoys out-glow the greyscale
and an albatross waits, blinking.

Storm whispers rise on the marine wall.

At the harbourmaster's mooring,
the Minotaur of Seas is lapping in sleep,
her ropes spread out in a bathtub of fog and brine,
resting in her wealth-water, waiting to carry again.

To carry out slaves under yellowed sails.

Those prisoners who sing their eyes out
and go blind with trying,
throats strained to the portholes,
hands on their necklaces.

A blue bell on the harbour side keeps calling.

Sounding out a history in unmade rains and guesses:
what the rigging tangles itself into,
what the starved come to as they grow tired of licking,
metal-eyed from moon worshipping.

Oh buffeted swan and seer of seas. Oh sounder of dink and clink.

The bird and the bell know what comes out and in
and at what hour sea cannibals come clean:
their skulls coming to an end on wooden decks,
the pop and gush of no-more-luck.

The ship will sing again, or sink. Sing, sing or sink.

PERIPHYLLA PERIPHYLLA

On and off,
it's the benign traffic light
of his coruscating heart:

a triangular jellyfish, spreading
and closing, visible through the greased glass
of the night bus. He travels

sunkenly and half happy
through a dawdling soup,
the city's deep midwater.

Aboard this electric ark,
his macaw-red eyes weep vodka,
a cell perishes with every blink.

He rides to his stop by the all night butchers.
All alit are the stripped shins
and beheaded hens.

When they dangle like that
they witness his troubled isosceles,
lighthousing through his body.

He walks on — possible
only by beating at
the krill-strewn sea.

In the ninth abyss
the tensing pipes of his bright organ
widen for water.

TURNING EDGE

Bomb hail pocks the newest snow.
Our breath on the indigo pane shrinks quick.

At a casual minus ten a brave break in the bell cloud
makes space in the spare pines. Between

layers of wool, down and fibre, flecks
of heat are stunned to sitting. For a minute.

Skillet-shallow sun suffixes afternoons:
another hour of light, no degree warmer.

When we talk we hammer tiny parts of ice,
nose hairs thickening on in-breaths,

brows kindling and glue. Inside: immobility.
Outside hurries us. Stewed in hops and herring,

waiting's tired. A late twist of winter refrosts
the wet edges, staggers the pools back into place.

AMY DE'ATH

◊ ◊ ◊

Amy De'Ath was born in Suffolk in 1985. She studied at the University of East Anglia and in Philadelphia, before moving to Australia and then London. Her publications include *Erec & Enide* (Salt, 2010), and *Andromeda / The World Works for Me* (Crater Press, 2010). She has another chapbook forthcoming from Oystercatcher Press, and features in the anthology *Best British Poetry 2011* (Salt). She lives and works in London, and is currently Poet-in-Residence at the University of Surrey. In 2011 she will begin a PhD in feminist poetry at Simon Fraser University, Vancouver, Canada.

SONNET

I believe a readable face as crickets
swallow gleaming buildings full of
living banking hearts,
I believe the grand ineloquence of
summer's glue talking to you as if
pink axes in our reach,
and you, a click-clack landscape now
your thundering hero-organs chime
a way into my laundry tub.
I believe I'm down with this for shit

is all we have to do to make our
cobbled lottery love
a project with no truth to bear, light-
ness of touch I haven't got

the calm and lovely air.

POETRY FOR BOYS

That the Joy will soon come and make you suffer!

I.

Lay low in the words of the wood,
very subtle, not immune,
lay down in the snow and incline,
you are rest enough and dowry,
in the lay and the spook of an age,
very poor, still glamour,
still further than you think even
more, from the day duly swallow,
to the real green day in the dream,
very full, cracking bough,
the undoing publicity of meaning
all the whole black sky is feeling
the screwing over, resin delight
delightful residual meaning, still night.

II.

I'm a weeping boy and a centaur caving in.
Adventures, find me—I'm hard to come by.
In the days when mirrors were made of burnished silver
I stayed up late,
in the nearly beautiful night I stood not quite

in the shower plenty natural and the water washed into
the time of my skin.
I imagined how to answer the question of whether
psychic malady is a personal affair. Then I wrung
my hair and dye came out.

If I had the money to dip in being a boy,
if I was Anna O., & fallen into autism or
steeped in prelingual glimpses of Lena's face,
I'd be living system: looped in my own elements.

A system closing talking only to itself.

III.

The house is full of dehumidifiers. Behind the house
a warm damp world enlarges itself, puffs
leaves and shelled birdsong along in it, and a baby crying
and deeds of courage.

If the sea is the swan road you can
appropriate the lake lady just by laughing.
You don't have to bed her to make her love you.
The ivy thinks it's English:
a swish of ermine reveals the last girl standing, and
she is sugary and she is foxy and maybe she is Jewish.
She swims the channel towards your parinage.

How will she mark her scent?
She's sleepy and reaches land and regulatory forest. She's sleepy.
Her leaf hair trails behind her with crisp packets.
How will she tend the steer?
How will she steer the wheel?

IV.

There is a boy who (I) cannot lose,
unbridled is he and of real flesh

by Spanish radio he and I were made to be.
And I, he not made nor ever been,
nor ever did I went with he, never
eat by such great lies or lied with
great intent, did I swim swim again
or consider praying men then give
my heart to all the boy in pasta-

O, hold me in the light.

V.

I turned 25 and my conception finished:
is my face
already the death mask, yes?
And not featuring lakes much anymore
and notwithstanding the 21st century,
and sitting, watching East Anglia shudder and insisting
never to have been an Angle!

Is a boy only happening
like this: carving out tuning forks
amenable sausage
recycled lovecats, acts of love,
a wireless odour of US coast,
its vintage blushing
overblown: yes, it's a boy

and I am a boy now applauding myself on the wet grass.
I give myself a peppered kiss.
I love the visionary earth-boys by diluted petty means like this.

VI.

Here we go, my legs blow back
into the garden, the latest late night
cicada store is so appealing I know
I will stay here till humanity ends.

Well it's tough, the greatest fish
mow close to the coral and
the friendliest cats say "hi" a million
as they slap your ass.

Say I stay, open-legged for the
summer, feet stuck firmly in the
Airtrain, a dewy idea peaking at what
is this vector I caress?
What ran my legs brushing
alongside the linotype, O Walty,
won't you sidle or trot smartly by
me, you are just a dog,
you don't know what it's like.

VII.

Down dampen sully unknown
because you ate the sunshine,
asunder among the porch light
a tune to know, of history's mesh
an epistolary flash of deer
young, always in fashion, in brave
pursuit, climbing down a piece
of fruit to get to the last boy in
town, who ate the town and
whipped his jacket up to the
wind and ripened on a cloud,
a compensating cloud in glut, and
he fell down, he fell upon those
vandals, he was a feat of sunshine.

VIII.

Boys and solipsists are written out and I pant for boys in
appellatives, I'd eat your hair and holes my God.

I call them puissant debtors and lavish roadies
or whatever you want.

I sleep in nature where warrens
serve as nail bars

I'm a stubborn boy and poised
at that beat replaced in love.

wherever my body takes precedence
I do not owe a boy, either.

it's like this forever

. . .

Wherever I am, Hello boy.
I do not owe a law, either.

INUA ELLAMS

◊ ◊ ◊

Inua Ellams was born in Jos, Plateau State, Nigeria in 1984. He has four books published including *Thirteen Fairy Negro Tales* (Poetry, Flipped Eye, 2005) *The 14th Tale* (Play, Flipped Eye, 2009) and *Untitled* (Poetry & Play, Oberon, 2010). His poems were included in anthologies: *Generation Txt* (Penned in the Margins, 2006) and *City State* (Penned in the Margins, 2009). His second pamphlet *Candy Coated Unicorns and Converse All Stars* is due out in 2011.

OF ALL THE BOYS OF PLATEAU PRIVATE SCHOOL,

the dry skinned short shorted dust dipped
disciples of Bruce Lee and Chuck Norris,
of all the wire headed heathen, my posse

of Voltron Forced, Fraggle Rocked, Teenage
Mutant Hero Nerds each had a party trick.
Kika B would eat a fistful of desert sand

spiced with soldier ants, chew till it turned
the beige mulch of Rich Tea biscuits,
swallow, twice, and live to tell the tale.

Dapo Mokoye could flatulate the first line
of the national anthem with such clarity,
Raymond Ogunsayo swore he heard words.

T could spit faster than fleas skip, further
than lizards leap, spit so high, we claimed
him Herculean in form, a half god of rainfall

and of the four talents, I was the art kid

awaiting the school bell. With the sun for
floodlights, the ground for canvas, a sharp
twig splashing through sand like paint,

I'd capture Kika's grin, Dapo's musical sin,
T's thick lips saliva dripping and me, angled
as a ghetto Van Gogh—shoulders hunched
to get the staunch slouch right. We'd pose

beside the drawing, sculptures of ourselves,
the other boys clustered, dark eyed, envious
but not enough to scatter sand in any way.

So this day after, we sidle into school, still
sketch-slouched, find our canvas suddenly
blank, sand—mysteriously smoothed . . .

Most likely the janitor simply did his job,
but instead we conjure how creatures of
the night, voodoo priests and priestesses,

mami watas, bush babies, witch doctors,
sorcerers, all the sulphur-scorched-glowing
-eyed-black-circled venom stuff rumoured

to work the night, we theorise they spent
their witching hour playing with our sand.
The priest outlined us in white chalk, spoke

in voodoo talk, raised up dust dolls of us
who, naked with the witches, limboed
with their brooms; bush babies gaggled

and gooed in devil glee till the clock struck
three, they vanished instantly, a foul wind
of howling wolves swept through, leaving

sand smooth as fresh sheets, as the wide
ruled page I dent, and I reminisce of tongues
turned tireless, of dark art's thrill, of how
quick we fixed our lil plight with fantasy

which flows, you know, ever shapes, ever
reveals the world—an unquenchable sea
of myth mist that wisp-whips whoever asks it.

Some trap it with tongues or a double bass
strummed, some turn its incline to sculpted
forms, a boy once enticed it with sand and
a stick or now as I do, with a pad and a Bic.

PORTRAIT OF PROMETHEUS
AS A BASKETBALL PLAYER

His lay-up starts from mountains
not with landslide, rumble or some gorgon clash
of titans but as shadow-fall across stream,
some thief-in-the-night-black-Christ
type stealth. In the nights before now,
his name, whispered in small circles, muttered
by demigods and goddesses, spread rebellious,

rough on the tongues of whores and queens,
pillows pressed between thighs moaning.
Men will call him father, son or king
of the court. His stride will ripple oceans,
feet whip-crack quick, back scarred,
hunched over and a silent storm about him.
Both hands blurred, scorched, bleeding
you see nothing but sparks splash off
his palms, hear nothing but breeze beneath
his shuck "n" jive towards the basket
carved of darkness, net of soil and stars.
Fearing nothing of passing from legend to myth,
he fakes left, crossover, dribbles down
the line, soars as if an eagle,
chained to hang time.

GUERRILLAGARDENWRITINGPOEM

The mouth of the city is tongued with tar
its glands gutter saliva, teeth chatter in rail
clatter, throat echoes car horns and tyre's
screech, forging new language: a brick city
smoke-speak of stainless steel consonants
and suffocated vowels. These are trees and
shrubbery, the clustered flora battling all
hours, staccato staggered through streets.

Meet Rich and Eleanor on Brabourn Grove
as he wrestles her wheelbarrow over cobble
stones to the traffic island by Kitto Road
where this night, coloured a turquoise grit,
cathedral-quiet and saintly, makes prayer
of their whispers and ritual of their work:
bent over, clear rubble, cut weed and plant.

But more than seeds are sown here. You
can tell by his tender pat on tended patch;

the soft cuff to a boy's head — first day to
school, by how they rest with parent-pride
against stone walls, huff into winter's cold,
press faces together as though tulips might
stem from two lips, gather spades, forks,
weeds and go. Rich wheelbarrows back to
Eleanor's as vowels flower or flowers vowel
through smoke-speak, soil softens, the city
drenched with new language, thrills and
the drains are drunk with dreams.

The sky sways on the safe side of tipsy
and it's altogether an alien time of half
life and hope, an after-fight of gentle fog
and city smog, where the debris of dew drips
to this narrative of progress, this city tale;
this story is my story, this vista my song.

I cluster in the quiet, stack against steel,
seek islands, hope, and a pen to sow with.

CHARLOTTE GEATER

◊ ◊ ◊

Charlotte Geater was born in Ipswich in 1989. She studied English at St Edmund Hall, Oxford. She was a winner in the Foyle Young Poets awards in 2005, 2006, and 2007. Her poems were included in anthologies *Stop Sharpening Your Knives* (3) & (4) (Eggbox, 2009 & 2010) and *The Mays XVII & XVIII* (Varsity Publications).

MORO

There was a bowl on your windowsill.
At first I thought you'd left them there too long
and that oranges could burn, like me last summer,
elbows caught out by the sun.

The flesh was purple. We swapped bruises,
comments on the news. Our bank accounts
were knee-deep in red. You listed locations, and all
I could think (Belfast) (Seattle) was

this orange is from another country (Italy).
Your fingers were too pink for March, each tip
like a thimble. There were charms falling

at your neck, and I, dainty and unsure
leaned over the bin and spat out three seeds
at empty wicker, like gristle, gristle, bone.

GROTESQUERIE

I taught our children tricks with rope, how to swallow
so many pennies that they sound like rough old keys

stuck in locks when they laugh, and they all eat pendants
that they can slip back up their throats when they get caught

in arguments. I brought them up for freakshows,
on Geek Love, now they breathe fire when they're angry

at me, they'll spit on the drapes and then it's all over
for another front room, another pair of hand-weft curtains.

We'd been saving up for emigration. Nicola's better
than a piggy bank, she can hide coins wherever and only she

can bite them out of nothing or blow a crisp ten into the gaps
between her quivering fingers. Henry still dreams of the World

of Wonders, says it's his world, that he only wants to work
in America, where people will watch him untie chains and handle snakes.

Samuel only speaks with his feet. Molly won't say what she dreams of
but she paints her body like she's wearing feathers.

No matter where we go, the ocean rolls out before us
and however many times I vomit small change, or eat

half an aeroplane just to practice, I can't propel us across the vast
unsteady sea, and people don't clap when I try any more.

NOT GOODBYE

so let's say you lose months. the skyline's been
torn apart, or it's winter now, only
winter. say they leave us ruins, lonely
with no motorways or A roads. within

our lives, let's say they paint something, the sky
or a small world is red where it wasn't before.
say they burn lands end, raze glastonbury tor
and break up the ley lines like they were shy,

sleeping, had wanted someone else to end it.
i will paint red brick houses across our walls,
fill the windows with blue, shout, take illicit
drives with you, try to smooth back the earth. all's

fair now. say you see it destroyed, empty, red;
say the moon falls overhead. all we keep is us.

SQUALOR

Fur crosses the backs of my hands
along the thin lines where there would be bone
bridges swaying in the swamp of my hands
milky from the moisturiser
smelling of broken coconut

I want to escape with you to grey gardens
where people transform into beautiful petits fours
mould circles their arms like icing sugar
dust smells as sweet as talcum powder
used instead of shampoo

we have crumbled from the dry white
of a dog's jaws
to the spit and fragments caught under his tongue

let's leave the house and go skinny dipping
and we can wash our hands and faces in the water
where we are just dirty blue girls
who live, hairless, under the sea.

DAI GEORGE

◊ ◊ ◊

Dai George was born in Cardiff in 1986. He has studied at the universities of Bristol and Columbia, New York, where he completed an MFA in 2010. Now back in Britain, he lives in London and works as a tutor and freelance critic. His first collection is forthcoming from Seren in 2013.

NEW TRANSLATION

Thanks to the hacks that still insist
on fixing the smallest glitch in Luke,
the Lord's Prayer can be gamely glossed
at the tenth line. No more is sin a lake
we're led to like bullocks on market day
but rather rum misadventure:
Save us — and here things get a little coy —
at the time of trial. So censure,
you will note, ceases to be the point.
Our trial will come, with a banal clunk,
certain as a night time accident
beneath the sheets of a novice monk.
Maybe the poor brother will someday learn
to foil his loins and be reborn

but the rest of us? I have a friend—
how to avoid fogging this with Greek?—
well, *she's seen our photo and seems not to mind.*
By which I mean, I've come into luck,
a jackpot by my normal standard.
Sloping from the corner, she lands
at a Siamese angle by my side,
by which I mean my clammy hands
anticipate her clinch. Am I being clear?
I mean underwear dilates as she roves
into smelling distance, that my pores
seethe with a pheasant reduction, cloves
and other odours of the lavished boy
who can't decide if he wants to try

the wares. I can't, then, but summon my first
speculative shots at courting you,
and your announcement, or perhaps your boast,
I willed against till it proved untrue:
I don't believe in monogamy.
Now, I had to approach a phrase like this
with a certain flexibility,
a feel for the deeper emphasis.
I translated it a handkerchief
fluttered down to commence the game.
By gradual, doting steps, the bluff
was exposed, we annulled that glum
and altogether too easy vow.
I may have to hold you to it now.

PLANS WITH THE UNMET WIFE

Should we first meet in a market
somewhere equidistant from our lives
and take up the tryst, slightly against choice,

69

in a city of mutual strangeness;
should lunch hour in a gallery
become a truant afternoon;

should I fondle you and grow privy
to homeland, or the childhood room
where you'd hide and which I'll never visit;

if we have to fly family over
for the ceremony, and tell them straight
that we've altered our bearing,

how is this going to work?
Aflutter from the thought a kid
of mine might be oval-eyed,

I pace Manhattan's narrow rood.
Our dark-skinned and bilingual girl
would be better poised, thank god,

than her old man. Better able to glide
thoughtlessly between her stations,
beholden less to land than tide.

Should people be landlocked, though?
Years from now, you're bathing her
in the sink of our apartment.

Something of the light: your shorter hair
and rolled sleeves have me in mind
of Nan, when she worked a loofah

every Friday against my back.
My parents' weekly respite:
packed off for an overnight,

I remember the peerless heat
of jimjams from the radiator
sliding over my shampooed head,

and the contours of my second bed—
how Mam was only separate
by twenty minutes of motorway.

METROPOLIS

Your oldest friend leafs a newspaper
in a café, far-off, copying.
He's taken residency for the day,
a monk figuring his manuscript,
pen-nib trembling. Steam mixes
with invading drain smells, burnt coffee,
the paper cranes of tensile thought
as he stitches another character.

Cherry blossom filters to the floor
or snags neon, or doesn't bloom
at all, save for the tourist gardens.
At times, you hanker for spousal rights:
permission to reject the proud,
delicate feats of male friendship
and be with him in Japanese springtime
where he fumbles into new alphabets
and each word is an act of lacework.

DISTRACTION DURING EVENSONG

And they with out taryinge lefte the shyp and their father and folowed hym.
Matthew 10: 23

Hard to say whether it was temperature or memory, birds
garbling through doors as they creaked apart to let
a late arrival at the back, or a high C that wouldn't merge
with the choral bulk. A marginal sharpness.
Something unappeased, clanging through the semibreve rest, an end
to all the usual comforts.

That afternoon the garden had gushed. The rosemary bush
preened in flower, scented as a wife's closet.
Labour for three hours in the young summer, a wish
granted and granted over with each shear and snip.
A downing of tools. A windfall taken indoors and sprigged in the lamb.
The walk to chapel newly showered.

Now more than tithing was required. An outright auction:
inessentials piled in lots, the life of flannels
and family, ready for the gavel. In place of life, action:
not whipping with birches and salt, but pursuit.
Leave now. Let the dinner burn.

Resuming voice, the choir whined beyond the lectern,
wishful voices winding through the air
like the first snore of a bedmate, a misunderstanding.

TOM GILLIVER

◊ ◊ ◊

Tom Gilliver was born in Harrogate in 1990. He studied English at Christ's College Cambridge and is currently studying for his Masters degree. He was shortlisted for the Faber New Poets Award in 2008.

THE GRAFT

The branches frame themselves, and in the chinks
they think. The dead clay that is so tired of thinking
is brought to light, and drinks.

I may remember this place, but the land
repeats itself imperfectly, and at the wind's hand
is forever scattered. Before, were there not
two men walking bent as if carrying news, and surprising
two pheasants at the wood's shaded brink,
where the path falls beyond
the sun's devising?

But I remember the sun, how it perplexed
the leaves; and I was perplexed, too,
though for a different reason.

And the wood remembered itself in another season,
which I had forgotten, and it was emptied by the thought.
And the thought found no body
but wood within wood, and there dug in.

Now it's cold. The trees shiver the snow from their branches;
it lands at their feet; they cannot move them.

THIS FEATHER STIRS

This is above all strangeness.
Upon the crown o' the cliff, what thing was that
which parted from you?

I lie still and am a shell among shells,
closed to the sound of wind-ruining:
I cup my ear to the ground.
The silt has nothing to say, and beneath
there is nothing molten moving.

Where the lip of each shell touches the sand
it carves a mute O, and no longer moves
with the tide, unless fierce,
or with the wheeling sky that stuns the land
and to it dizzy nothing proves.

The thoughtful land grows faint.
Division by zero brought forth this deceit,
an abundance of nothing:
and the tide's token, an abeyance of shells —
its shiftless body, its shining wet receipt.

TALKING BACK

May all through the wood, and the curlew
   by the by. As if an unsolicited reply.
Water it? Besides, it rains
   upon the thought: as if to rinse away the stains
   the earth's spin cycle leaves.
Shuffle to the middle and re-assess.
More beautiful than its depiction, so I claim.

Yet more lovely than all these, at the edge
   of the reconstructed hill, some feet
away there are weeds going without names.

BEFORE WE THAW

With one finger on the atlas,
Bella traces the confused outline
of *Nova Zembla.*
She says it is as far up as you can go
without turning to ice.
She says it is where icicles come from
in the night, and where reindeer go
to hibernate.

Beyond the window torn paper is falling,
   filled with mistakes
and sketches and drafts.

EMILY HASLER

◊　◊　◊

Emily Hasler was born in Felixstowe in 1985 and studied for her BA and Masters degrees at Warwick University. In 2009 she was awarded second prize in the Edwin Morgan International Poetry Competition. Her poems appear in *Dove Release: New Flights and Voices* (Worple Press, 2010) and *Best British Poems 2011* (Salt, 2011). Her debut pamphlet *Natural Histories* is forthcoming from Salt.

CAKE FORK

An instrument unseen to him before now. It sent the soft shades
of the lowlight back yet softer. The idea was simple to grasp:

the cake, the fork, their proximate places at the table. And easy,
to clutch its delicate bodiless limb, lever it against the outside

edge of his index finger, to jig the light upon its joint with his
large thumb. He takes it to the cake, its scalpel finger investigates

the sponge. Already it is part of him—a branching—itself deltoid.
He bites, deliberately clamps his teeth, testing its qualities,

the temper of the metal. The echo of a pain calls. A glass bell rings
from a room at the top of a wide staircase. Already he fails to imagine

this instrument before he was shown to it, before it inclined to the roof of
his mouth.

WET SEASON

"*Pictures of nothing, all alike.*" Hazlitt on Turner

The world is like nothing we have ever seen,
the catastrophe of the morning's rain
hangs in the air and will not be drawn out. Yet, light.

On the horizon that has forgotten itself
and the water that refuses to own its depth
there is light.

A lone crawler toward light—
his back like a beacon on the road—that frog
that refused to budge, like light through eyelids
he sat in your mind, crawled into the space
behind your smile and sketched himself beyond your eyes.
We speak pictures of nothing in silence, quite unalike.

And the rain falls on.   Scrape, blot, wipe wet paint,
draw over. Nothing can be undone, draw over, paint on
until the canvas turns in on itself and is pierced
                              by a hole, a flame, a lake.

THE CORMORANTS

You scan the bay and always see one—
plumped like a discarded coat on some
purposeful post of sea-bleached wood.

Oil-black, slick—yet slightly scragged
around the neck, set down without care
and ready, because there is no space

no then-now or here-there
except that which can be flown through
or dived into with a half-jump

to go deeper, to precisely grasp fish,
water snakes, small eels. If you could see that,
if you could see them underwater,

being a different shape,
then this world would not be as it is.
They cry out to the city leaveleave

or nothingisasitseems. Offcuts of night—
for the night is made of them,
is when they come in squalls to the coast

and rest outside your window.
Your hair dried wiry with salt air,
you pretend not to notice them,

watch TV. They're there again in the morning
appearing as hastily hung hats.
You see them extend their necks, preen themselves

or they stand spread-winged for a second
blazon onto your eye like a motto
—you point one out to me,

say, Ilovethecormorants, they are alwaysthere.

ON READING THE MEANING OF "FALCHION" IN AN ENCYCLOPAEDIA

A "falchion", from the Old French
is a sword. It cuts swathes like the Persian scimitar
and digs through bowels as the Chinese Dao does.
But it is its own, itself: a sword, from the Old French.
A specific means of death.

The incision that was made becomes apparent
and blood hurries to the surface after the mid-air cartoon pause.
The stench of blood undrying. Battles rewind, soldiers come to life.
And what you were saying was that people were dying
on the end of this particular kind of knife?

Knowledge is the great unstaunchable wound.
A sword is a sword is a sword. But
what sort? And a word, yes, means nothing by itself,
is simply a point which impales, pins a specimen of reality to the paper
so we might squint and imagine how it once flew.

And now they're everywhere, and when someone wields the word
I hold my hands up. I say, yes, a sword, from the Old French. Yet before
I must have run through many pages, escaping harm, not knowing
the pointed syllables had sharp edges and that I scanned so close to danger
and failed to notice the sun catching at the quilloned crossguard.

OLI HAZZARD

◊ ◊ ◊

Oli Hazzard was born in Bristol in 1986. His poetry has appeared or is forthcoming in magazines and anthologies including *The Forward Book of Poetry 2010*, *The Best British Poetry 2011* and *New Poetries V (Carcanet)*. He studied English at University College London and is currently a graduate student at Bristol University.

MOVING IN

You take me down to the crease in the hills
Where the farm's boundaries are smothered
By brambles and the dry stream bed lies
Like a pelt—we follow it quietly, shoeless,
Listening to the waves at Calpe knead into
The beach, and reaching out my hand to
Touch your hair we are suddenly
Aware of the sensation that we are being
Overheard: yet all there is on this side
Of the valley is the fuzz of telephone
Wires overhead and darkness slowly
Encroaching behind the skin-pink clouds—
The orange trees, after all, seem to clutch themselves

Above the safflowers and alfalfas that
Spring from the ground like cocked eyebrows —
So, stepping onwards — stalking, by now —
Convinced that night is simply the folding over
Of fingers, leaned into a steeple — we hunt
For some burrow, some hood of earth
Where the sound of the sea is as unbroken
As it is within a coiled shell and build
A fire whose voice, like chicks-being-
Incessantly-hatched, will make our
Own seem all the more improbable. But
Now, as I sit alone, crumbling dry leaves
In my palm, it seems all I can dream of is
The onset of sleep. Really, I hardly notice
The rising heat of the circling brush fire that
Flays the whole sky of its stars.

THE INABILITY TO RECALL THE
PRECISE WORD FOR SOMETHING

"All things are words of some strange tongue"
Borges

The first person you see after leaving your house
One who always wants to know what's going on
To make money by any means possible
A surgical sponge accidentally left inside a patient's body
Given to incessant or idiotic laughter
An incestuous desire for one's sister
The act of mentally undressing someone
One who speaks or offers opinions on matters beyond their knowledge
A secret meeting of people who are hatching a plot
The act of beating or whipping school children
The categorization of something that is useless or trivial
Belching with the taste of undigested meat
One who is addicted to abusive speech

The use of foul or abusive language to relieve stress or ease pain
The condition of one who is only amorous when the lights are out
To blind by putting a hot copper basin near someone's eyes
The act of opening a bottle with a sabre
The habit of dropping in at mealtimes
The act of killing every twentieth person
One who eats frogs
The low rumbling of distant thunder
Someone who hates practicing the piano
The practice of writing on one side of the paper
A horse's attempt to remove its rider
The collective hisses of a disapproving audience
The sensation that someone is mentally undressing you
The act of self-castration
Being likely to make a mistake
One who fakes a smile, as on television
Counting using one's fingers
The act or attitude of lying down
The smell of rain on dry ground
The space between two windows

Source: http://users.tinyonline.co.uk/gswithenbank/unuwords.htm

ARRIVAL

The vibrating harp of rain drove them
sprinting into the pine wood. Made content amongst shadow
and cicada trills, they soon grew fond of the names
they'd given to the trees and animals; in night's recesses
they learned to conjure mephitic
fumes from the bomb-puckered earth,
to sing certain obscene songs;
they ran through the wood
trailing honeyed light behind themselves,
their songs wholly eaten up by silence.

Yet the stubbly meadowland drew them out one evening;
they crept on their bellies to avoid being spied,

dug their fingers into the pliant earth at the sound of
fires. The empty trees, having clutched laminate sky all winter,
suddenly sprung meat and wet clothes on their branches
(pale stars blinked awake in the gaps between) —
and until the dawn leaned over the mountains
(their rigid eyes twitched from their stare)
the extended branches of the air
carried murmuring voices far into the night.

BADLANDS

There are no trees in the yellow foaming
Wheat fields; or maybe a single, gnarled
Birch that, Lear-like, webs the air
                  with its waving limbs.

The pylons stand bow-legged, mercenary.
The wires slither towards the horizon
Bearing whispered prayers. The sky is bright
                  and taut, bruised with space.

A man, as naked as if dressed in his own pelt,
Cartwheels in the nest of a cloud shadow.
I call out to him, but his stride is unbroken.
                  I read my letters.

The sun disperses its light like a lozenge: —
Its sediment quivers at my feet. I cannot
Withhold my crazy laughter as my voice
                  sieves into the wind.

PRELUDE TO GROWTH

Tomorrow is watching today through the one-way mirror.
Something is taken from each, exchanged for something else, more
or less valuable.

Your too-thick glasses, the ones that
are totally off-trend, render the suddenly swarming pavilions
a tearful furnace.

No-one is more or less orange. Microbes of sand grow
on my eyes. The collision between cement mixer and ice cream van
provokes less identity

in the etiolated gallantry of longhand. Make milk my measure
of white. Or today a smaller fraction of my life.
To oil that lends water a gradient.

And yet the gorgeous weather continues to move along
the walls,
plucks the Dijon telephone, approves its endurance.

Now your hand hovers
over each object: it self-inflates to meet the bruit gift.
As these beaches

remain leaning into their own portrait,
in that fuller night, our skin powdery, we see the whole event
unfolding very slowly,

the wind somersaulting down our throats.

DANIEL HITCHENS

◊ ◊ ◊

Daniel Hitchens was born in Oxford in 1989. He graduated from the University of Cambridge this year with a degree in English. He has been a Foyle Young Poet of the Year and a runner-up in the *Times* Stephen Spender Prize for Poetry Translation. He was a founding member of the *Pomegranate* editorial team.

FRUITBOWL

You sense the delicate borders of sleep
drawing down the curtained-black room;
again, the incline and the loop

of floated images, jigsaw dream
logic, the hand-held surface that lurches
to half-lost memories—unlit landscapes from

childhood: infinite fields of firs and larches,
transparent lakes circled by crowds,
felt in the quiet, as the dead in churches,

and leading on to masked lies, false charades,
hazardous diversions: the lost jumble
of remembrance that remembering erodes.

Awake is the place of the precise fruitbowl
with its predictable contents. Your back
arched into the sofa. The wait as you fumble

for the light. Fathomable things: the book
calmed on the table; the birdsong now flown;
cupboards standing shut while you blink.

The sudden comfort of being alone
at night, with not a noise except the screams
of foxes, cars down the lane,

people you love murmuring in rooms
above. You stay on the safe side of that line.
Satan came first to Eve in her dreams.

FIRST SHAVE AFTER COMA

Squaring up to the mirror,
he shuffles through
greeting an old enemy,
hand shaking on a knife edge.

He re-emerges in the glass
while clods of rain pile up
in the bathroom panes.
The year had nearly buried him.

Outside, the garden is featureless,
the grass yellowed, he imagines,
by the heatwave under which
the town has been breathing for weeks.

from **ELECTION 2010:**
A POETIC REVIEW

TED HUGHES

When the Labour Party dropped Clause Four
Crow was furious.
Vomiting up his intestines, he wrote a very stern letter to Tribune.
God refused to publish it.
"What a loser," Crow remarked to the bullfinch
Who was disgusted by the woodpecker's thumping.

The ostriches had invented a new form of sewage
Which yelled all over the wronged obesity of the forest
Shouted its head off into the filthy ground
Screamed at the desensitised pines
Until it got a sore throat.
They called it "Politics".
Then Crow smashed a plank of wood over Alan Milburn's head
And Philip Hammond drew a policy statement out of his navel
And the putrescent Scottish Nationalists coughed up globs of blood.
"I'm definitely voting Green next time," Crow thought.

PHILIP LARKIN

In the vast blaze of monitors they stand
And almost think themselves normal blokes,
Before a soundman signals to begin. So
It comes round: the mirror-worn-out jokes,
The traffic jamless journeys, the unplanned
Presented infants, the tamed claps. All know
That they are going to die: knowledge that fills
Each Cabinet meeting, neither sinister
Nor unseen; and yet the Minister
For Business, Innovation and Skills

Knows this is one thing that can't be reformed.
I watch them ignoring it. We
All do: what else is to be done?
No good to think of how the memory
Returns to times when significance yawned
And not the rest of life: the things begun,
Abandoned, left as static as cement.
I remove my shirt in front of the debate.
How cold it gets at half past eight,
How soon the time is melted down and spent.

PERCY BYSSHE SHELLEY

I weep for Gordon Brown — for he is dead!
O Labour, on whose red rose I have gazed,
By whose pale gleam my spirit has been led
Through lightless caverns and grey mists, and, dazed,
Through this weak world as one who questions Truth
Not vigorously when in a polling booth,

Now hear me! To an inbox have I come
Where, like Proserpin in her ruined Fame,
Who wandered in the fields bereft and dumb,
An emailed memo lies. It reads: "My name
Is Ozymandelson, king of spin: Cower,
Ye Tories!" Power, hast thou lost thy Power?

SARAH HOWE

◊ ◊ ◊

Sarah Howe was born in Hong Kong to an English father and Chinese mother. She studied English at Cambridge and Harvard and completed a doctorate on Renaissance poetry and the visual imagination, also at Cambridge, where she now has a Research Fellowship at Gonville and Caius College. Her poems and reviews have appeared in magazines including *Shearsman*, *Horizon Review*, *PN Review* and the *London Review of Books*. Her pamphlet *A Certain Chinese Encyclopedia* was published by tall-lighthouse. She won an Eric Gregory Award in 2010.

A PAINTING

I watched the turquoise pastel
melt between your fingerpads;
how later you flayed

the waxen surface back
to the sunflower patch
of a forethought, your

instrument an upturned
brush, flaked to the grain—
the fusty sugar paper buckled.

You upended everything,
always careless of things:
finest sables splayed

under their own wand's weight,
weeks forgotten—till, twirled
to mustachios, they emerged,

gunged, from the silted
floor of a chemical jamjar.
I tidied, like a verger

or prefect, purging
with the stream from the oil-
fingered tap. Stop,

you said, printing
my elbow with a rusty index,
pointing past an ancient

meal's craquelured dish
to the oyster crust
at the edge of an unscraped palette—

chewy rainbow, blistered jewels.

FAULTS ESCAPED

I wake to a sodium forest. Passengers
      speed through intensifying haloes.
      The bright underpass thirsts tonight.

In shuttered factories machines hum on
      & daylight shakes itself out. Imagine
      mounting over the corrugated world,

imagine how it arrows: one upside down
      eye after another, snatches of heaven
      in a misted spoon. Then they are gone.

I like to listen for the gabble of surfaces—
      all summer the dripping walls, the wind-
      blown gate unable to stop. They say

belief is a comfort. Still the whispering
      as the ants dismantle every flaw, insert
      themselves in cracks like keys, all summer,

and how the wet grout crumbles tonight
      into honey & all my pretty tiles lie slumped.
      The shopfront trembles in its shutters.

Night is a veiled and silent mother;
      a living cave, the stirrings in the sides,
      water pushing blindly through a stone—

each cold diamond determined to be born.
      Too soon they leave, their love a bloom
      of salt; those encaustic tears, the stars.

CROCODILE

Over the years they had had many similar meals. The starter
was a chilled pea soup, its oddity just enough to hold the atten-
tion; that unexpected cold, spreading in waves over teeth and
tongue. At that moment, the blunt end of his spoon connected
softly with the table. The evening light skewed down from the
high-up windows and glittered off a hundred knives poised to
cut. Maybe she was thinking how quickly the summer would

go from now on. He feared that she would leave him and said so too often when they were alone. She looked down at her napkin, then up; in that second, when no eyes met, it seemed perfectly right that words should be things you have to digest. Why had she had to say it? He imagined all the conversations in the room pouring from their unknown protagonists as though from the excised stomach of a hulking and battle-scarred crocodile, an eighteen-footer dragged straight from the Cretaceous. When the triumphant fisherman tipped up that membranous sac, out would gush an uncontrollable bilge of fluorescent green goo: he watched it swilling across the restaurant's parquet, chuckled as the tray-poised waiters skidded on their windmilling hams, so many Michael Flatleys. As the reeking ooze receded, the diners became aware of diverse objects beached between their corroded chairlegs: asymmetrically polished stones, the barb-stripped calami of ibis or other broad-quilled waders, one rifled musket's intact silver flintlock, a small girl's hand, an acid-dinted comb.

CHINOISERIE

I said *Sleepy Willow*. You said *Voiture*.

That was one of our shorter arguments.
My hands twist inside your sprung hands

till we feel the lack of the smallest human

mittens trapped inside them—squirming rose,
a nest of looping ratlets—such petulant joy.

Imagine a dustless mantelpiece (we'll call it

The Past) where rests a tiny, puzzling globe—
feel its chisel-riddled crust—like the preciousest

of golfballs, forgot on its rosewood tee. Look,

it's actually twelve concentric ivory spheres which
all spin freely, whittled by unimaginable hands

from one elephant-smelling hunk: a machine for doing

nothing; a dragon's pearl that's rolled away. Frailest
of armillaries, whose star-dinted, independent heavens

turn on the innermost yellowing pea—shall we name it

This Misbegot Earth? Some nights you comfort
me with sterile knuckles, your nibbled nailbeds

ragged as the ghost of a motheaten tux. You

remind me of our lost chimneysweep and
sometimes it's too much—nose like a leaky

spigot, moppy brow. His long-necked gestures.

You sing to me of machinists—how even in sleep they
sentry a watchmaker lathe, imagining themselves

in strobe-lit celestial factories, holding an ink bloom pupil

to the closing eye of a vernier scale, balancing
an atom in the aptest calliper. Anxious wives watch

their somnolent hands, turning tools to invisible wheels.

ANDREW JAMISON

◇ ◇ ◇

Andrew Jamison was born in Co. Down in 1986 and educated there, at Down High School, before studying at the universities of London and St Andrews. He has been selected to represent the UK in Rome at the 2011 *International Biennale of Young Artists* and currently works for *Teach First*, teaching English in Bradford, at Dixons Allerton Academy.

THE BUS FROM BELFAST

There is nostalgia deep in the very bolts
of these steel seats outside Europa central station
which, here, this evening, sit me down and make me face
the evening, face to face and bus by bus,
as bus by bus sunlight falls out of love with Cave Hill
and leaves me here nostalgic, wondering
what there is to love and what nostalgia's all about.

And there is disappointment deep
in the mayonnaise of my chicken sandwich,
my return ticket, the holes which are developing
all through my jeans and Converse, the sigh
that comes with sitting down which, also, is developing

as disappointment and nostalgia spray-paint themselves
onto this journey home; which is itself a city

in a way. And there is melancholy too,
deep in the come-and-go of this whole place
behind the laughter in the pubs and parks
and in the rush to cross the road and open doors.
And everywhere is everything. And nothing
comes but every way that nothing can.
And by "this whole place" I don't just mean Belfast.

THE STARLINGS

Everything, relatively speaking,
is simple: a tree a tree, the sky the sky,

the clock on the wall the clock on the wall,
a tick a tick, a tock a tock, time time.

And then come the starlings, tearing about,
beautiful obliterations of the commonplace,

going through the motions
of their unchoreographed air show:

tremendously alike,
tremendously alone.

DEATH'S DOOR

after Jorge Guillen

I've been mulling it over
this now-and-again they call the future.
Because it comes to me: this door, ajar,

a chink that lights up some corridor
through the last house, last street, last quarter
of some lost city. It is a silent corner.

Someone remind me it is summer,
this — a gin and tonic, each finger
already numbing round the tumbler.

THINKING ABOUT THE POINT OF THINGS ON A SPRING EVENING ON THE KILLYLEAGH ROAD

Sunlight shows up the dirt on the window —
bird shit, streaks of rain-stain from an over-night shower
put the pristine white of the PVC frame to shame —
a Belfast-bound flight disappears into Belfast
flares and unflares in the soft blaze of a spring evening
like a second sun, or a one-off star
through this one-off, belter of a blue sky
as it's radioed through its last approach
touching down to a province of "politics" —
we'd call it something else if there was a word for it —
untouched by the in-your-face canvassing,
the prospect of door-to-door campaigning,
the lecturing in the electioneering
that's going on and is ongoing now
as lampposts wear placards of touched-up,
photo-shopped, yet puffy, pasty-faced politicians,
cable tied, fastened to streetlight after streetlight
by some fastidious, unpaid recruit, with hope:
busybodies, do-gooders who've got done over.
MEP's double chins belie their à la carte lifestyles —
scream "foie gras to start, fillet steak then the cheeseboard;"
a taxing regime of lunches on tick to the taxpayer —
there they are, beside words like future, your, vote, for,
the same old same old from the same old-timers

while buccaneery young bucks bear the look of the duped;
dimpled, malevolent grins of hard-liners,
the streets of Crossgar are festooned with them,
wherever you look—left, right and centre—
like a festival without the festivities,
festivities without a festival,
or come to think of it, a festival without a festival,
but their greens and their blues will fester and fade
in the elements, the heat and the rain that will fall
through all the Baltic founderings of an Ulster winter,
rare days of summer's sun-split trees, heat-woven lull,
as lampooners, gossipers, small talkers
lampoon, gossip and small talk it all up in their blogs.
Here, the chickens, however, take it all in their stride
as if the world is one big joke, a cakewalk—
I've been especially impressed by the rooster;
sometimes I wonder if he has seen the future.
My father footers at something in the garden,
someone says something unimportant in the kitchen
to my mother's usual, love-full clatter of pans,
rattled to within an inch of their life,
the *Hollyoaks* theme tune comes from the living room
as loud as you like, as if there was no tomorrow—
you cannot hear the tick of a clock here—
ironically, you wouldn't catch me dead in there.
And tonight death seems like a million miles away
as I, perhaps, get closer to what it is I want to say.
And tonight the world feels like a million dollars,
and I feel the need for words like shebang,
arpeggio, carpaccio, Caravaggio,
piano, allegro, pimiento, bravado,
and in the garden everything seems so
abandoned, so easy-come easy-go:
the watering can has fallen on its side,
the daffodils are here, there and everywhere,
the spade against the ditch—a loner,
the deflated and faded Gilbert rugby ball,
unkicked, undrop-goaled, unconverted, un-tried,
tired, it lies beyond my brother's jinking,
dinking, running-rings-around-me, scoring,

reminds me of the games we used to play, one-on-one,
garry-owening, chipping and chasing
our life away on an evening like this evening,
thirsts slaked by big pints of Robinson's Orange Barley Water,
a pause in play before we'd sidestep each other
until it couldn't get any darker,
(older now, perhaps to grow is also to outgrow;
older now, we find ourselves homesick at home)
as now my nephews' Disney slide is folded, horizontal
on the patch of grass it will keep from the rain and kill,
and beside the pampas grass beside the greenhouse
the midges seem left to their own devices:
a swarm of small sun gods hovering en masse,
up to no good, a swathe of sunlit nuisance,
and the robin, alone, skitters through the Leylandii
from one branch to another branch, inching,
shaking then steadying, shaking then steadying,
and I, for the life of me, can't tell you why
but remain gobsmacked at its balancing act,
its light-footed, easy-does-it, there-there, now-now knack,
the quiet science behind its body's equilibrium,
its give and take, tightrope walker-like suspension,
which makes me see an order in the world, a system,
and think it's not so bad, it's not all doom and gloom.
And so, birds yap all through all the ash trees
as evening burns into the back of my head, recedes,
and so it is that I weigh things up, catch myself on —
second suns, one-off-stars, robins, Leylandii —
caught up in all the catchings of the eye.

ANNIE KATCHINSKA

◊ ◊ ◊

Annie Katchinska was born in Moscow in 1990 and brought up in London. She was a Foyle Young Poet of the Year in 2006 and 2007, and is on the Pomegranate editorial team. Her poems were included in the anthologies *City State* and *Voice Recognition*, and her Faber New Poets pamphlet was published in 2010. She recently graduated from Cambridge University, and currently lives in Japan.

THE TWENTY THIRD MINUTE

Supple, tender,
   you skitter the pitch,
something is licking your calves and feet,
you are good,
you mean well but all around you
a great glue of bees smeared red and white
        and whistling,
rippling, a fabric-and-boot smell,
ecstatic cameras,
microphone fizz,
   the song of your country on salty tongues,
everything's there and it drips,
yes,

99

all they ever taught you
drips down your neck
so you shed it,
running at no one,
for no one—
she's singing in your ear, just think
if you took her hand she'd pull you into the earth,
its core a bird skull
nested in liquid and crust,
sparked
to your heel and shimmering,
shifting beneath you, beneath
the foreign scream
that's a faceful of tropical spider,
beneath the green spilling out to a swamp
your fists and knees batter,
beneath the strips
of thin white alligator
you skid over,
this is the same hot anger
you felt in the childhood jungle of pubs
when your uncles hollered
and told you to pray
and you swore this, swore only this
so now
the grass ticking
the men pour down
you turn beggar
Give me
Give me magma

BLUE

Trojan, I think of you with boulders and innards
and gods criss-crossing your eyes.
I live through days of silence, orange-yellow cheeks
and lentils eaten with a wooden spoon,

remembering the bedroom and the red of your palms
the days you couldn't understand blue,
and waited for a summons—the air you called a shield
would glitter into place
and hard sun collect in your hair, your lashes,
the corners of your mouth. Your blue
is every clink and clash and stab, cold jewellery clamped
to every joint, cold insects sweating in your hands
looking up at the slab
you called bronze, and tried to shine back at
with your blood-smeared sticks of sky. I think
of your body pouring over me the colour of midmorning;
and now
as you trip
I think of clouds across your chest,
clusters of smiling gods in your eyes as you gape
at what falls as blue rain.

TONI BRAXTON

My fate was a weird surname and lipstick that glowed in the
dark, and adults who slurred, "Russia! Russsssia!" at video
cameras every year. My parents pinned carpets to the walls
and bought a tape recorder, gave me bad asthma attacks with
Beverley Craven, Ace of Base, Enya, more Enya. Crawling under
the table at dinner parties retrieving furry gherkins and measur-
ing guests' legs with a tape measure, I thought Red Square was
full of onions and we'd never go home, and I wanted karaoke
not two alphabets, a frog in my throat like Toni Braxton or
the woman from M People. The song played simultaneously
on Capital and Magic until one day I heard she had to stop
begging her heart to be unbroken or her boobs would explode,
true story I swore, as somebody's parents filed for divorce and
somebody else burst into tears in another room saying they
only ever talked to carpets, by now drooping off the walls in a
tragic fashion and smelling of gherkins. Say you love me.

FEBRUARY

Tight, tight skin, and the room rings. It matters.

This is February, so she dissolves
smiley faces of vitamin C in oceanic
glasses of water, eyeballs herself and thinks

tendon

tetanus

optic nerve

and someone visits and juggles everything in the fruitbowl
even the grapes, but she binds her face

in white scarves, smears marjoram on her hands. Her
eyes are stethoscopes, her lungs
broken harmonicas, she sees
each minute as a grain of brown rice

laid out on a table, death locked
in scummy bones and staggers
upstairs to Google -osis, -osis!
join the dots between

her skin crackling under cotton, rattling
beneath bracelets of eczema, camel-shaped bruises, bitter moths
and the dirt on the window—

the world glows, glows.
Watch her
check her fingertips for flames.

ANDREW McMILLAN

◊　◊　◊

Andrew McMillan was born in Barnsley in 1988. He studied English Literature with Creative Writing at Lancaster University and is studying for an MA in English Literature at UCL. A debut pamphlet, *every salt advance*, was published by Red Squirrel Press in 2009. A second pamphlet, *the moon is a supporting player*, is due from Red Squirrel Press in October 2011.

from IN MY DREAMS YOU WALK DRIPPING FROM A SEA JOURNEY ON THE HIGHWAY ACROSS AMERICA

I. ATLANTIC CROSSING

a man in "departures" made
an Arthur Miller script of *goodbye*

his wife whispering how *it is only a month*
some men in history have slept for longer

tomorrow's rain huddled
beneath the plane

England unravelling
into the Irish Sea

II. SHIPS IN THE NIGHT

I saw Ferlinghetti
he looked like an eccentric trainer
                              of big cats
and carried the weight of a small island
                              in his breath

no sorrow is so bad   Lawrence
                              as that which quite goes by

IV. CHICAGO

this has been

the sun was the face of the man
in the American Gothic painting

a waitress had a voice like cold coffee
the day sweated

the day wrung itself out and left
itself to dry between the streets

a homeless man played jazz   pigeons scattered
into the iron rafters of the El Train

VI. NEW YORK CITY

squinting eye of the streets
wind moves like an elegant dress

down the backs of young men   sweat
makes new peninsulas

the half light of a corner deli
a man running with a bouquet of flowers
the last hope of the city

NABOKOV'S BUTTERFLIES

savage/beauty of pinned wings
hillsides stalked with suit   pipe   net

glass encyclopaedia
of specimen
                    thousands

frail arms crucified   skin tone lingerie
draped across thorax   nerves

                    think of
a wife   pulling pages from the embers
                    coming back from the brink

innocence is only innocent if we long to touch it
but don't

innocence is only innocent until it falls
                              fogged out of trees
until someone pins it down
spreads the limbs
and names it

6:30AM

sleep had been singular
so long
that   on waking next to him
I felt like the submariner resurfacing
amazed to find the world survived
with so much air
such tundra of sky

OBITUARY OF A LESSER EAST-EUROPEAN POET

a sturdy toby jug of a talent
will be remembered for the four lines

> *the violence of chrysanthemums*
> *the snow choked distances*
> *I mourn the curve of the earth*
> *bending towards spring*

people hadn't heard his work
but they heard him whistling

through the backrooms of the village
where he waited out his life

he liked trousers to look worked in
he could hold a tune in a storm

his death was overshadowed by a power cut
and a rare win for the national cricket team

he is survived by a country which ignored him
and a wife whom he ignored

SIOFRA McSHERRY

◊　◊　◊

Siofra McSherry was born in Northern Ireland and read English at Christ Church College, Oxford. She took her Masters at UCL and is currently completing a PhD in American Studies at King's College London. Her poems have been included in *Birdbook* (Sidekick Books, 2011).

L'ÉTOILE

I find the veils are dropping by the hour.
Petals dry and curl and fall from me.
First things I imagined to be ours,

then hair and skin and all the rest of me,
down to only bones as cold as roots
of the cherry tree that flowers in January.

Most of me has gone to brute
cold like birds in winter beds.
I am searching for a quiet place that suits

the scattering of bones, the sowing of dead
seeds on gunmetal ground,
to find entwined in the cherry roots a bed

where sleeping tiny-hearted things are sound
asleep like stars in deepest cold.
I tried to drown

my bones in the heavy waters that unfold
beneath the greying ice on the canal
like a frightening story told

on freezing nights in winter. Fatal,
the watching crow comes hopping down
to redistribute the moon, with a ritual

clicking and reshuffling of moon bones
by beak and wing until winter is redressed
and I as far from yours as from my own.

FAUST

I have you at the summons of my pen
my Mephistopheles, for your sake I have robbed
the landscape of its colours with greedy eyes
rubbed its pigments into the shades of your skin
illuminated your face in sun and stone
and your eyes with the calf-deep colour of sea on sand.
I have conjured sudden birds, a flock of white
spreading your smile across grey stormy light
and from the trembling tendons of the rabbit
coaxed the ghost of your uncertain kiss.

What shall you fetch me, for what unseasonal fruit
should I send you flying, my expectant creature of cloud?
I would have you race to see the world for me
brushing the joints of continents with winged feet,

diving into heavy foreign air
and out again and back to me to sing
with a stormy tongue your songs of all the world,
in my little room shake out the patchwork globe
before me with your voice and weave with air
all the glowing silks of seas and skies.

But it strains the mind, keeping you in flesh
as a shell's spiral tightens towards the dark.
I would almost have you take another shape,
animate the bared bones of desire
and have you clatter thus goat-shod to me
through the quiet suburban afternoons.
My windswept spirit's allegiance is to air
and he keeps company with unfamiliar clouds.
Waxing monstrous, crowned with cumulus, my devil
dances up a storm with discordant feet
and empties himself of meaning with the rain
      as the banks of cloud are emptied by the rain.

SLEEPLESS

     In the spring the uncertain sun
stepped down and shook us awake. My body
was pinioned in bright sleeplessness
                 through March
                 April,

praying that my thoughts should catch
in the soft hollow where
words and pictures burn, a match's
black scalloped lick across them.
Dipping like a fish towards it feeling
the relinquishing slide, always
bobbing back into silver night, scenery
     slipping back into the skull.

By summer I thought of it as a hawk,
oil slick talons and feathers sharp
as if painted, and under the talons there
a small bird broken with black wounds
sprayed across the breast,
a white breast and a spreading dark,
wrenched out of flight and here brought
to the particular beauty of a dying bird.

Around the seeping black
of the hurt spots the days catch and flow,
the clear light waters learning
to be afraid of dark.

TO A BLACKBERRY MAGGOT

Glutton.
Still, I can't blame you
for taking the fattest and
best. We would do the same,
nibbling sideslant through
the sweetest parts of August.
For all your jawing and your
wriggling there's plenty
left to pink the fingers with
and purple the tongue.
Scratches, nettle stings
and tears belong to those
who value inaccessibility over
firm-to-finger blackness, when
pressed revealing claret—
these maggot-free remains
fall easily to the hand, settle just
as brightly on the tongue as all
those shining higher
in the hedge like eyes of crows.

BEN MAIER

◊ ◊ ◊

Ben Maier was born in North London in 1987. He studied English at Durham University, before completing an MA in Creative Writing at the Seamus Heaney Centre for Poetry, Queen's University Belfast. He currently lives in Belfast, where he is studying for a PhD on "radio poetry". He also works as an actor and musician.

GONE BABY GONE

Your Epiphone stands sentinel by the sink
like a lodestone leant against the draining board.
It faces the fridge, which is forever on the blink.

A plectrum, on the table where you left it, is caught—
immovable as a collector's prized relic—
on a plinth of sunbeam from the skylight.

Certain sounds are echoed in these things: the clicks
of the catches on your guitar case for instance, or
else long notes rising from the cellar, where the acoustics

were better. The wind chimes above the door
softly ring out your return. Innumerable
are the prompts of grieving. The kettle boils for

the umpteenth time, and what it boils down to is this: one vulnerable
song, now lost, now here, now almost hummable.

GALL

"A gall . . . represents the growth reaction of the host—a plant—to the
attack of a parasite . . . and develops either by an abnormal increase in the
number of plant cells or by the cells becoming abnormally enlarged . . .
Whatever its form, a gall is derived wholly from the tissues of the host plant.
In no sense is the parasite the gall-*maker*. It is the gall-*causer*"

The Pocket Encyclopaedia of Plant Galls in Colour, Arnold Darlington

Sing
of a home within the song
of something else • of going hunchback
on a strange seed • ghosting the oak
and goading the sprung twig • cuckolding the acorn
self-kettled in the seed's keep • to warn the warp of the unborn
bark • spin a fiction of the carrier's scaffold • of the sap
stream • feel as tale teases out tale • as radiators tap
tunes • to cloak the coital jut of story • the kick
and crease of filament • a prolific ache
a kenning • a filigree film of wing
sing   •   gently
sing gently
the sting

A SHORT HISTORY OF TEXTILES

Chapter 1 of *A Short History of Textiles*
is devoted to the qualities of cotton.

∿

In Chapter 2, a cursory glance
is given to hospital sheets
which once began life as great swathes,

not King- but Continent-sized,
over which sharpened iron grids were laid

to cut away the standard shape:
large enough for the average man
to turn over twice.

∿

Chapter 3 tells how silk warps, given water or salt,
and so would never do for sails.

∿

And Chapter 4: how the public learned
to make do without the linen maps
which were once so common,

those fabrics of hinterland and frontier
outlined in black with oak gall ink.

∿

Chapter 5 relates the biography
of Joseph Marie Jacquard,
who watched as his son

was shot down at his side
and who later developed

the Jacquard loom
which occasioned the necessary loss
of so many jobs.

∾

Chapter 6 concerns itself only
with the lucency of sun through lace.

∾

Chapter 7 is dedicated to the presence
of *appliqué* in the work of F. Scott Fitzgerald
and his part in its meteoric rise in sales.

∾

Finally, Chapter 8: the parable of the boy
assigned the banner making for the parade,

who having neglected to read
A Short History of Textiles,
inverted the colours of the flag

and was justly chastised
by all of his fathers.

LAURA MARSH

◊ ◊ ◊

Laura Marsh was born in Bedfordshire in 1989. She was a Foyle Young Poet in 2005 and 2006, and was a runner-up in the Christopher Tower and a winner of the Rialto Young Poets competition both in 2007. She studied English Language and Literature at Christ Church, Oxford and currently works for a documentary film company.

THE WINTER EMPRESS

No need to pause on a stalactite. Beaming
she showed everyone an athlete caught mid
high jump, embarrassed the private screams
of big-eared bats with glowing eyes. She slid

in with the rain. Colours dripped from her cheeks,
made the room pink and our hair flyaway,
shocked into the coronets of chic
girls drowning, fanning haywire. She came to stay

like a replacement for silk. Thin ice.
We take thick furs and salted streets on trust,
forgetting, and hooked on far off goodbyes
that replay, attracted with the charge of dust.

We hold hands and crackle. It is never night,
only snowy static, the persistent thought
frosting over everything. In her light
we flicker through channels, always dawn.

MISTAKES IN CLOSED CAPTIONING

You're the horse and I failed.

You will trample
a too-narrow bridleway, not looking
where you are going, where the broken glass
is trodden into pheasant tracks by girls
with nicotine eyes, who set fire
to aerosol cans. Mud will splatter
your shins to theme music; on the A-road
I'm hurrying down, squinting, you will pause,
yourself again, as something I misread
returns to you.

You look worse than I feel.

RELICS

I have walked through catacombs wanting fear
to strike me, and I have not understood
the relics of saints. For even the good:
their bones remain although they disappear.
But in Love, you say, we do not outwear
our bodies as we might, that if Love could
begin with hair loosed to the breeze, it should

extend itself through each part it comes near.
Then farther it stretches to more than just
the nerves, so that we feel with parts of us
already dead, or the clothes we are in.
We love with senseless nails and thick skin,
you say, till what a lock of hair undoes
we feel with the bones that will come to dust.

THE WIFE'S LAMENT

You said once, nothing will come between us—
less of a promise than a barefaced fact
of our matter. Easy back then, intact
and you, all brawn. We hardly thought it was
the hardest that would endure; the minus
what we'd sensed with till we were inexact
as fog. We two, rolled around with winds, cracked
atmospheres apart. The trouble with us
was anything. We were never supernovas.

APOLLO'S HYACINTHS

Not much of a courtship, this afterwards love.
I come by Tuesdays to the allotments' gate
in my best coat and scarf, and watch you shove
bulbs into the incipient soil, and wait.

We barely speak—gardening gloves, cuttings, shears—
but what you give me, I can make do with:
those days when the low sun warms my ears,
and you bend across with your spartan kiss.

Yet, come April, your cheeks are touched with triumph.
Festoons lie about you, bringing the glory days
back from the underworld. Then mine the "hmph!"

of being planted in the wrong place,
while you cherish your unrepeatable trick,
the bloom in your heart that no one can pick.

ANNABELLA MASSEY

◊ ◊ ◊

Annabella Massey was born in 1989 and grew up in both England and China. She studied English Literature and Creative Writing at the University of Warwick. She is currently working in Japan and will be applying for a Masters degree in due course. She was a commended Foyle Young Poet in 2006 and her poems have been included in *Panado* (Tower Poetry, 2010).

A GIFT OF LILIES

These lilies don't last, shedding stamen
across my desk. I accidentally smear
an orangery across false grain; I take

my own fingerprints when I reach for a sheet.
Difficult not to crush / cuckold
so many little sexes
with a cough or flick. Yellow petals break

loose intermittently, their skirts unwinding
as lazy weaponry
        the old axis weakening.

These lilies are in my room
and so they have forgotten you, though yes,
they were your gilding. But for the past week,
I have been exchanging and re-exchanging

oxygen with nine golden horns (the metal
transmuting into limp skin, clinging against my own).
So they have become myself; they could tell

anyone what I seem to be when I sleep.
Tear open a discarded petal,
release my own molecules and dust.

There is nothing wrong in flowing
towards nothing as these stamen do.
A head is really only for show and their stems

work well, sucking the limescale up
like dye. So let the trumpets coil

and sneeze orangery instead of sound.
The flowers were this week's gift   and all is welcome.

ISTANBUL

Here, tulips daub and streak
(half dipped in dye)
each filled by (or pregnant with) a small, slight
sun. And they spilled here
first: no windmill ever required to leak

the nectar; to powder heads dry
on each scalloped grind;
to claim gifts twice; to slake
clear stamen clean with nail.

Just keep these streets
well: you have new silk,
new cashmere now. You saw their threads swell
over door frame (lighter than heat). Pleating
your Istanbul in with this web. Wetting the mesh with ink.

ACTRESS

I.

Here, seawater isn't full of plastic at all,
but jellyfish: rainless, crinkled discs.
Perhaps they solidify waves, make peaks
bloom thicker. Today, you've gone

to Princes' Island for horse-drawn carts
and the charred silk of unwanted harems.
At breakfast, we ate bread (though I discover
you cheat, finding diet pills on the desk one morning).

You had seeded rolls with sour cherry and cheese.
By night, you rehearse your lines as you sleep
chivalrous little love   chivalrous little love
slurred whispers saturating the rafters above   sending the script abroad.

II.

Sending the script abroad to saturate his mind:
words and photographs to sluice working cells,
slake his brain so it rings golden and still.
Then to gild a steeping inner skull
                    your secret goblet.

But we clink ordinary glasses over dinner,
forks unfolding mackerel and dark leaves, soft as clover.
Drinking pomegranate juice

                  instead of wine.

III.

Pomegranate juice instead of wine —
even when liquid,
                I can taste kernel
and seed. Morning, and the street heaves
in the sun; heat slung back to a flightless sky.
You dab makeup on, blending a base from

a bluebottled vial of eye-drops, rollers
which massage the face; Elizabeth Arden's
eight hour cream, thick
and smelling of white hickory and tar.

One glass jar of Tiger Balm. You need
this second face to channel your script;
to lift and sunsplit on cue; to arch in light
sifting tortoise shell and camera lens;
to make him remember and want.

IV.

All day, we remember which bracelets we want.
Turquoise against silver; onyx on silk. I slide
stitched ore across my wrist, I take this weight
under four o'clock sun and you say: *I'm in love*

with mine; it makes me want to learn chivalry.
We each fill our old goblets and drink,
fingers pressing the bone. Feeling for bruises,
linkage, buds. Checking tarnished temples

for gold. Yes, we've been absent.

                              Miles abroad,
an Icelandic volcano slews. Tidelines
fossilize around empty brims. Young
landscapes stiffen under salt. And over coffee,

we continue choosing which women we'll be.
Words like *authority / formidable* are snagged
by wind and taken into the creasing sea.
Raked even flatter and eventually, broken
down like weed. Dregs fill up

most of our demitasse cups; half done,
we have to leave the grains alone, settling
like blended sand and treacle. Breathing
through foam. In the harbour, we see birds

landing on a cellophane strip: they nearly sink.

JAMES MIDGLEY

◇ ◇ ◇

James Midgley was born in Windsor in 1986. He founded the literary journal *Mimesis* in 2006, which he edited until its end in 2010. He holds an MA with distinction from the University of East Anglia, where he is currently studying towards a PhD. In 2008 he received an Eric Gregory award.

BUTTERFLY ANTENNAE

after Alexander Calder's "Antennae with Red and Blue Dots"

Tonight there is too much interference to think.
In a town's scattered Rubik's cube of televisions
one face is switched to static.

≈

In a wood of slow electrical pylons
sparks of butterflies
make it difficult to think.

There is the brain's confetti, as if shaken
into the air by a petal-headed child.

≈

I heard of a man who was lighting a film set
when a hawkmoth mistook his ear for an escape
and writhed against the eardrum's straitjacket.

≈

Then it was always raining, even on the train,
where a fly caught against the window
travelled the length of the country like a rumour.

We travelled weeks in search of the wind's bellows,
a slack-cheeked god,

our progress overseen
by the moon's persistent surgeon's face.

≈

Locked in my palm
the butterfly loses itself amongst my fingers
and the hand knows only chalkdust.

This is how the word butterfly was first absorbed—
with the rubbing of palms, and prayer.

≈

Tonight all thought is interfering.
I never shook that intruder loose, a rhythmless drummer.

The rain of untuned radios
is swarming

above the buildings, over the river
which is a shifting mirror made of craneflies

125

with so much to observe
it has shattered its attentions.

PORTRAIT OF A PIG

The pig shifts
as a mugger wind rifles it for possessions,

possessing a particular love
for bristles like the sproutings on an old woman's face.

And though totally devoid
of motor function, the pig

turns and snorts
like a lawn sprinkler. Fst Fst.

I remember heaving a pane of glass indoors,
the thought of it fluid between my fingers

but the weight substantial
and all its parts eager to strike out on their own.

This is to say the pig is an untenable thing,
possessed of a mind no more constant

than the mathematical values of Θ,
here deducing the curve of a folded snout.

Oh I am tired of saying what this pig isn't!
But the pig is no artefact of cinema,
antique animation of a zoopraxiscopic camera

and the pig is no glimmery anima
endowed with a butter-slathered body.

And though the pig hangs its head
over a wall, this beast is no amulet

against a falsifying spirit.
Space is the pig and here the pig is.

THE INVENTION OF FACES

Do you remember the invention of faces?
Someone does but it's no longer me.
These celluloids washed against the beach
like the deaths of jellyfish.

Remember the boy lifting food to a mouth
and finding none,
grapes shed upon a board before him,
a fish looking surprised.

Remember the woman combing her hair,
a mirror making a display case of her features
and the brush's needles knowing and reknowing.

So the eye bloats
and the sun's atavistic orb flexes and focuses.
So the mouth is an apple's afterthought
and looks but has no way of looking.

Recall with me how it was before:
silhouette and knife edge,
the hand's uncanny language,

another way of meeting, as acrobats under the lamps.
I don't want to be human any longer.

HARRIET MOORE

◊ ◊ ◊

Harriet Moore is from South London. She has recently graduated from UCL with a BA in English Literature. She has been published by *Magma* and *Clinic* and recorded for *PoetCasting*. She now interns for a literary agent and co-edits an arts blog.

from WHALEFALL

I
WHALE

Blood clouds in the wave, it rains for hours
This is my blood, my rain   I'm pouring

In the blue holes, through sea bowels
Sieving the whole Soul of the World
Through my skull, pushing myself into its corners

Blubber overflows like rivers when it floodrains
I am foraged, a forgotten field of skin
Things won't grow and are mudstuck,

Bloodbanks cave in, seams drop-stitch rotten landfall
Wintering bodypile like a whole orchard of apples

Dropped trout. My brain's   unhooking
This is how you gulp quicksand, how you tell safe hands to let go

Below watertight wound of sky and sea I am heaps of
Unskimmed stones heavy with lung, waterlogged
Sinking slugging shores of stone homing towards more stone

The bookend marble basin of earth, flint on flint, my heart amongst this
Fold of peach; battering against earthskin, split chins

On shark teeth, afterbirth, graveyards of gills
I move boulders of old bodies

Snout-nudging for the finish line
Flag in ice, the last stop first sleepwalk,
Beginning of being air

There's this great weight I've been carrying round on my
Shoulders, there's shedding that must be done
An unpacking of my humpback, the misery
I've been storing up like fat

Men dream of opening me up, men dream
Stretchmarks of the underworld like rings in oak,
The wormholes, the teethcasts, the crooked bones;
These are the bruises I'm left with—the birthmark love-marks—
Patches of darkspace clinging to more dark
Like trees scarred by lightening, lands torn apart

Torn apart, I am mammal showers, fleshy downpours, last storms
It'll take years to shrug yourself from my thunder,
Months of mothballs radiators sunbeds towels
What is this pain? This bloodrain, these hours of leaking.
Like an old house, gaffa taped, walls falling into the garden
A tear duct, miles away, pulses through sand calling my name

So ripples grow and become something less dull,
Something throatlike. Water-voices, watered down
Shouts, mouthfuls of spectre, they stay eardrumming
Gravesong pulling towards rain

And more rain hours of it. Bloodpools. Breathless.
This is a soggy world. You won't get dry from it,
From this scrapheap drowning in your own skin,
You won't get dry from my saliva, I lick bones of the world clean
Before I let the flood in, before I bring ocean to my wounds like
Hammering death holes in boats and doing nothing

A blackhole tidal wave tent of skin freefalling finally cold-blooded
I think of all the water colours, the landlubbers and wait . . .

Halfway down now

It takes time, this process of dying. This timeline of being
Chopped down, a forest of bones scattering themselves:
Poplars and firs, the darkening bark of scapulas,
The foliage of ribs. Someone will collect the wood and inspect it

Before quietness, there are murky coastlines, places so dark
You don't know who you are, forever night time in this empty space
Before the tongues come and take over

In every season of water, there is something different, someone you once
      knew
I go through each feeling and try to touch it
Daylight, Midnight, Twilight, remembering it and forgetting and
Being still

BOG BODIES

I

Outside you all grow older,
Have a change of heart, move house in the summer.
But underneath, faces build on centuries of lost teeth
Canine, wisdom, raw molars, rotting
Jaws crisscrossing like jackdaws in woods.

Lost count of how long we've been here.
Can't tell a daybreak from a duskfall.
All I know is that I love you, enough
To deepfreeze, to rust, to plug my ears with dust.

Wrapped up in bedcovers of earthy water,
We dream the mud of the bog, the dud of the wetlands
In our blood; stranded corpses scared in the pest house
Of young love, drowning in dirt, untouched, un-dug.

Somehow the animals don't find us; can't claw what's left
With fake nails and blindness. Can't even smell us.

We survive under the landscape. Dog flesh, skeletons gone
But still there somehow underneath the peated eiderdown
Of the dead years when we don't speak.

Repeatedly pulling earth over our shoulders
We are neither water nor land, storm or stillness,
Like fishes that sleepwalk on mountains, horses that don't drown.

In a dampbed we wait between realms.

II

Winter came like a cough caught in chests.
The ground froze around us.
Wheezy, breathless, still becoming bog, we half-lived,
Half-forgot. A rib cage here and there.

A front tooth. Not a lot.

Not everything I touch is lasting.
Not even bogland,
Not even men.

He got up and walked away washing his clothes,
Scooping the dirt from his eyes, unsheathing himself from
Bogteeth like a wet dog after rain.

Only I remained. A set of eyelids sewn shut. Dreaming of mudsling,
The land being torn up.

III

Spring. We are scalped heads. Lonely bodies,
Separately skulled.
I couldn't pull myself up behind him. Disturb the sewage of trees.
The flood of quietness around me.

So you all grow older without me,
Have a change of heart, move house in the summer,
Leave me to imagine in the dark.

Hip bones, kneecaps, thighs,
Outgrown body parts,

What's left is enough, you can rub it between finger and thumb,
It takes time to shrink wounds. To dry blood.
To knock seasons from the soles of your feet.

I let the bog hold me until I'm ready.

THE SHIP OF THESEUS

On all fours, at the shore of winter,
I check treebark against swatches, bloodtesting trunks for tombs

(I dreamed this deadwood ship, flotsam mausoleum
of dark-fish making my way down the Styx one fin in front of the other,

this is where I lost my voice. Knee-deep in larynx crossing
gangplanks back from the edge of the world, homeward in the dry-rot of
        dark

we have strayed further apart than I ever imagined, there is a deeper place
        but
I haven't found it, the aftershocks keep coming in with the tide),

once I had deep blood, it thins with every fell,
veins wasted sampling newborn forests
for timber to replace bone

shin twigs, right down to quicksand of marrow
where it all began, everything kindling, or tidewrack, matching bloodtypes
with shrubs.

You would not believe how long it takes us to lumbar puncture oaks,
to sift branches for the right type of spine,

only two thirds done, husk of ship, shallow grave,
and he's beckoning me, arthritic,
the driftwood ferryman with a fist of souls.

HELEN MORT

◊　◊　◊

Helen Mort was born in Sheffield in 1985. She has published two pamphlets with tall-lighthouse press, *The Shape of Every Box* and *A Pint for the Ghost*. Five times winner of the Foyle Young Poets award, she received an Eric Gregory Award in 2007 and won the Manchester Young Writer Prize in 2008. From 2010-2011, she was Poet in Residence at The Wordsworth Trust.

PHOTOGRAPHY

As if a single cord of wind
blew through your ribcage,
looped around your heart,
the photo catches you.

From now, your movement
is a kite's: you have the sky
and yet you're tethered
to a man below, an ancestor

who looks on plaintively
as if from an old print:

your face in his, or his in yours.
Even when he yields the string,

he's set your course. The breeze
may interfere, but you're directed
by a subtler thread, like all the living
anchored by the dead.

AGAINST SLEEP

I

Why does the dreamer breathe so hard?
Because he's running all night long
up brittle mountain paths

past one-horse seaside towns
he longed for as a child. Observe him:
still but racing through the dark

towards a long forsaken house,
an avenue of once familiar trees
that never welcomed him.

II

Sleep is an auditorium
with five full rows where nobody
is clapping. You have to enter

naked, cold, your breasts
like two grey stones. You have to
leave your things outside;

that lock of hair, those coat buttons.
They will be counted, weighed
put back exactly as they weren't.

III

I knew a man whose sleep
was almost murderous, his left arm
slung across me, tightening

round my neck, the way a python
surely works its prey.
I'd think about those sows

who gently roll onto their litters
as they lie, how love, at last,
must take our breath away.

IV

Sleep is a book where you can't
turn the final page, a film
you've seen before reduced

to one dark still; a girl
who hunches at a tabletop
as if to write or weep.

And if the page ever worked free,
the name rose to your lips, then
would you ever wake?

V

My mother slept like Jesus
on the cross, her arms flung wide,
her feet *en pointe*, her head turned

neatly to one side, a certain
slackness in the mouth
that comes with martyrdom,

there being no-one left to tell
about your final sacrifice,
no listener to apologise.

VI

Sleep is a rehearsal for the way
we'll drown. Each night,
we let it hold our faces down

our mouths miming an O,
our hair spread out, like kids
who fall through barely-frozen lakes,

their hands outstretched, their eyes
shut tight against the cold, or staring
at the arm that let them go.

A CHASER FOR MISS HEATH

At seventy, our dance mistress
could still perform
a perfect *pas des chats*.

Her French was wasted
in the north. We stood in line
repeating *parr-durr-shat*

or sniggered
as she waited in the wings,
her right hand beating time

against her hip, her eyes
avoiding ours. She never
made the stage.

It took me twenty years
to understand. Alone tonight
and far from home

in shoes that pinch my toes
until they bleed, my back
held ballerina straight,

I wait as she did, too afraid
to walk into a bar
where everyone's a stranger.

I almost see her glide
across the city night
to meet me, tall and white

and slim. A step behind,
she clicks her fingers. Elegant,
she counts me in.

CHARLOTTE NEWMAN

◊　◊　◊

Charlotte Newman read English at Selwyn College, Cambridge, and she has an MA in Modern and Contemporary Literature from Birkbeck College, University of London. As well as a brief stint indexing the entire back catalogue of the *Erotic Review*, Charlotte worked as a theatre critic for the Edinburgh fringe festival and was shortlisted for the Allen Wright award for young journalists in 2006. She writes regularly for *Poetry Review* and Salt's *Horizon Review*, and she reviews classics and fiction for the *Observer* and the *Literary Review*.

DANCING PRIZE

When Salome sings, the air
feels cheated. The chance to stare
limb on lung, the one compressed—
flung scrim like dragonfly dressed

in breathlessness. Where below,
unshriven, nomad-mad: "Know
how hair clings blood-wet when dead . . ."
sings the air with heavy head.

ALL THAT JAZZ

Duff credit card exact size of visor.
Nothing to see/hear save for the slattern
scurry of slutty children, neatly boxed
centre square; parental advisory
cusped by husbanded blinkers. The kids cling
to dad, judge in the High Court of Lahore,
whose credit doth abhor the things his kids
once wore. Much more like you, who, then unstoned,
fleshed Al-Jazeera hip-wise from our side;
your side mere forbidden fruit for the weird
men leering from the window the wrong side
of the car stuck stubborn in a non-pro-
verbial rut. Maximise the freedom
of uncovered eyes: turn flesh into hard pulp fact.

STILL BIRTHS

I. STREETLINES

Suffix softens the ending of things.
Day as antilyric in the paramour pages,
staring an age like a clock
          while one thick drop of I-know-you-not
troubles the windows of shops.
Fall of an edge—it's an art . . .
          had not the heart to disdain the
      typography.

Look at me with a livid lure—all
      flesh-wounds of the new season,
all brim and matter.
                  I leave a "kiss" on a phone line,
you wait winningly a week to leave
                  a low-slung chord of a histrionic.
          Not a single guttering line—just a whirred

warning compromised by the cocksure glance
of a mattering morning;
the gripe of the flattering dark.

He grows resilient to grappling rhymes,
stipulates time of the leavening beat—
I feel I fall on hard times;
flesh-fights with the real reason,
and in terms of elegance
it jars
with the tar on the heels
of our happenstance.

And I know lust is the hollow
in the bird's winging,
I am ordering a miracle to
look me in the face.
Cling to the mermaid's singing and
a blank cheque,
find the wreck among the reeds,
though the sails never raised;
write a "serenade". Find a parlour maid.
And write me your name in the dust

II. HE SAID

"I long ago lost a hound, a bay horse, and a turtle-dove, and I am still on their trail . . ."
Henry David Thoreau

"Lose something every day . . ." came the answer smilingly at him
across the crooked teeth of half a century.
And shaking, shook them loose; then it was searching, then it was art.
But beyond the ice and the pigeon blood paint, the exact
measurement of a lake's depth, the blunt fact of the spade's apology,
the philosophy sunk deep like a tone in a hymn:

I think, I think I believe, therefore, I am here, in this wilderness—
and I reason, therefore I squander and waste.
It is vast this transcendent space; I like it so I cut down trees

and craven my own image, I carve and I tease
the bark in twain and sell its soul to kindling. No speed, just haste
for my friends (you see I see solitude in this)

I rustle up a fire and a calm; a genial laugh and a whisper.
Some wine, a prophecy, some time and a spitted spark;
and all the while my eyes on my lake, my prize of the natural mind—
the beavers flinching in the half-lit wind,
my company a slow steady fake, a comfortable man in the dark
of the mind, of the chatter of the transistor

radio. Oh, no, I have skipped like a child—so ahead-of-myself.
I look at her not-yet-taken-photograph
and will her with me: among willows, among minnows (oh, she would
like that) I believe; could conceive of nothing, could
not fathom the depths of her innocent absence. By chance, her epitaph
is here with me. In bed with the trees; on the shelf.

III. TREPANNING

—the inverse of that.
I am glad, my love, it is not; pure mimicry of mimed hate—
So. How, my *talitha cumi*, go you by me?
You are young, too young by inches
to spell out a mercenary eulogy.
An arrowhead on a sexton's grave, you are
too far down to utter up song to your mouth,

I see all. Cannot trip me up with a thumb-wave.
Behave shame-faced in the quiet of the womb and its rim,
the shadow of him in its axis half-deafened;
defined by a mourning swim.
Though it has been said, some may think of Jael, she was no better than
a Trepanning Hussy . . . (OED)
I say, you lay with me with my hammer and vice; fetch me water—
sustenance, sense of entropy.

You can find me: naked, given, in a riven guise,
            or wise. I have no claim upon grace; only eyes, in place of
    tears.
You: give up a scapegoat, or cut out the throat
            of the wandering dew—
You: forgive. And as dawning arcs into morning
            all will lie dry, quite dry, only child
                    and as snug as a desert can be.

I see by me that you should not be—
            not the form of the thing;
not its fossil-like form.
        You are swallowed by tides, by *insides*; you are hollowed and warm;
            May you sleep there, lie fallow, and *mattering*.
Live long to fear the rigs and the water
            galvanised, the shuttle of a subtler sea.

RICHARD O'BRIEN

◊   ◊   ◊

Richard O'Brien was born in Peterborough in 1990. He is currently studying English and French at Brasenose College, and has worked in Nantes, France as an English language assistant. He was a winner of the Foyle Young Poets of the Year Award in 2006 and 2007. His first pamphlet, *your own devices*, was published in 2009 by tall-lighthouse press, in the Pilot series.

ISTHMUS

If I've been burning bridges you're the opposite,
and even saying it I'm frothing at the mouth,
a child with a lisp you tried to drown.
There's only so much you can water down
before there's no more parts per anything.
My friends said I was your peninsula —

hooked onto you, a camera strap tucked through
a loop that would go flying if you jogged too fast;
they told me our attachments would erode,
already were before the waters rose.
I told them it took years, slow as fingernails
and waved my hands, both bitten to the quick.

Peninsula. I rolled the word across my tongue
like toffee, tried to make it stick. It sounded like
what you'd end up with if you took enlargement pills,
or scribbled in your room and had no social skills.
It wasn't that. It was an almost-island, hanging
by a thread, the one I pulled out of your scarf

one Wednesday afternoon, and you slapped away
my hand, Obama's fly, and swore so fiercely
I thought the silk would tear, and said:
I'll never get this kind again, this shade of red.
They sell it everywhere. You got your scissors out,
a fate or fury, I'd forgotten which. Over my head

your silent sulk closed up, and I went drifting
in the regions where the ships get lost,
where planes fall into plug holes in the sand,
like when my mother let go of my hand
and Tesco towered round me, bright as Troy.
You told me you were tired of analogies.

I tried to kiss your neck. You said *Don't start*
and stamped your carbon footprint in the hall.
A puddle's deep enough to drown a man. A cigarette's
the thickness of the line, and you're all out of cigarettes.
The snorkel and the rubber duck won't help. I mouthed
Peninsula, and rolled onto the wrong side of the bed,

the gap between us cold as any sword. And as you slept
I tried to run my hands across your strata, find the place
where the foundations split and left me free but floating
far from shore; then, feeling continental, tucked my chin
behind your knee and tried to make it fit. It never did.
We'll soon forget we ever touched at all.

MOSES IN MEDIEVAL GLASS

A mistranslated manuscript
whittles a *halo* down to *horns*,
and serves to show
how quickly definition slips
when all that's left is outlines, forms
we lost the knack of bending back
the tongue for.

Half-opaque, a window
leading into something else,
as an optician clips
a second lens over a blurry first
and flicks — *one two, one two* —
until you can't be certain
which is which.

And you, turning your nose
before a kiss as if you turned
the pages of a codex
with your vellum palms,
pursing your parchment lips,
you think of the conversion
of twelve calves and pause —
you know that there's a boundary in this.

CONFESSIONS OF AN ACCIDENTAL ARSONIST

How can I say what made me miss the embers
as I came to you, bun-heavy, fingers derelict with yeast?
Our sheets that night were warm as plague, a pie crust,
and I felt your sleeping ribcage rise like loaves.
Outside, they didn't know our names, they turned
on spits of fitful sleep, but we were golden.

                    Slowly, love, we burned.

That night I dreamed I walked along the wharves.
The stars were crumbs, or fish too far away to catch;
the air played Chinese whispers, double Dutch,
kissed me with salt it rubbed into my elbow crooks
that stung like creaking timber, and a vast
sense of my littleness broke over me. I remember
        the stories. Light in the east.

Our daughter reads incendiary books.
The wrinkles kneaded in her face are politics,
the new astrology. Her crossed eyes are a crucifix
and her virginity reminds me I will die.
I stroke her inky head. Her hair invents the match.
The rotten weight drowsing across the roofs
             lifts its head like a latch.

Now something is rising in this half-baked city;
the morning light does a roaring trade, sold on
until every street is a red hand holding
another hand, the Thames a boiling butter churn,
the houses dribbling new red humours. Look.
The future kindles cupolas and kilns and bricks.
        We jump. Too many cooks

will spoil anything. That much we've learnt.
Blow on your fingers, shake off flour and slumber.
Now the news joyrides the wind. Unnumbered
wooden dotages collapse, choking, and the river heaves
a red hot vomit. They are counting casualties.
My lungs breathe in all the ash of London, and it sticks.
        I breathe out, but it sticks to me.

RICHARD OSMOND

◊ ◊ ◊

Richard Osmond was born in 1987. He studied English at Queens' College, Cambridge and is currently studying for a Masters Degree in Creative Writing at the University of St Andrews. He was a Foyle Young Poet of the Year in 2005 and his poetry was included in the anthology *The Mays XVIII* (Varsity Publications, 2010).

FOR THE NONCE

For the nonce = (?) for the particular purpose; or, more likely,
a gap-filling metrical tag with no meaning.'

R. A. Rebholz on Wyatt's "A Paraphrase of the Penitential Psalms"

So, lo,
once upon a joke there were two prawns or a cow
doing Shakespeare or a globe-eyed lime green squid
with a moustache or whatever psychedelic flora
spills and sprouts neon backwards out of the laugh. Restart

the song of a twisted idiom.

He is coming, my beloved
to sound a yarn of frayed edges

and the scattered ear; timid roebuck
flee like ripples to the word and my love
makes them dance

or rather rank and file under the crook of seeming,
just as the farmyard trudges into order
and cow and pig and chicken all
spend their upturned sense in carotid gushes,

just as, before Solomon, before, even, that bastard Solomon could have been
but wasn't,
          Wyatt's David, with Barsabe the bright, dissolved

in a metrical tag, all lineage lost to the pick-up and punch,
the great tales of rock and sling heaped in
with foreplay, fumbled buttons,
the comedian's tired preamble; all flame, all song and substance
sparpled for the nonce.

BAIT AND SWITCH

    Kekulé's familiar,
    genius of the benzene
    ring, spat out its tail.

    I dream green electric
    under the bed,

    snake,
    I'm pulling out the furniture
    when you flicker like
    a buzzing fluorescent and the rat in your belly
    swallows
    you whole or you shed your whole
    self like a slit skin.

thrashing prey snake in voltaic
seizure, strobing between fang
and fur, rat heart hum and rearing
coils, flight-flattened, back-bent,
spliced to strike, crying

let me catch you

my radical hieroglyph, abstract of
the sublime Javan frankincense

lend me the musk
to speak the unpronounceable

fragrance of your broken
ideogram, then,

my greasy lover, your lost tongue
in my mouth, the venom.

KUNSTKAMERA

a plaque:
"Tsar Peter the First
valued science
over sorcery"

a diagram:
"the replacement of eyes
with glass marbles"

children gape,
roughly incant Latin inscriptions,
hydrocephalus,
a swollen head,
polydactyly,
seven bleached beansprout fingers.

pale, vinegared,
seven-limbed lizard.
a fork-necked deer,
both heads startled stiff, branching,
as if encircled by wolves
or witches.

brined babies, brains removed;
hunched, crippled crescents held
shelfbound, unborn, age-lined, arranged
by date, unnamed
by Peter the Great, who,
one Siberian solstice,
caught the mandrake phases of the mutant moon
in eight glass jars.

ANATOMIST

science in the bones and chime
of names, you cast the knitted strip

over the nape of your *collum*
because friday is tie day as sure as the norse
love goddess is sunk like haddock
in the deep fat

and we must abstain from flesh.

fresh from praying the nerves
of the upper limb in mystic latin,
you list your drinks
with the solemn technic of your art,
as if somewhere between Smirnoff
and blackthorn is a word
to rhyme with the sweet tang
of the kiss
on my neck,
which you have forgotten.

VIDYAN RAVINTHIRAN

◇   ◇   ◇

Vidyan Ravinthiran is a research fellow at Cambridge and a lecturer at Oxford. His pamphlet, *At Home or Nowhere*, was published by tall-lighthouse in 2008; other work is anthologised in *Joining Music With Reason* (Waywiser Press, 2010) and *The Best British Poetry* (Salt, 2011). He reviews regularly for *Poetry Review* and *PN Review* and is currently working on his first poetry collection, his first novel, and an academic monograph about Elizabeth Bishop.

MA

Confused as the blue avatar on the big screen
you hiss *is she speaking English?*
over our shared popcorn.
Scared only of escalators and fish
you should be driven through every council estate
exploited by the BNP, speak to the people
from your own Popemobile, enlarged to accommodate
the pillowy softness of you, liable to spill;
even the office bully who mocked your pidgin —
Calvin and Klein, legless tights, I'm a spring bird! —
sobbed at the reunion when you hugged her hard.
You say when you first came here it was snowing;

as kids girn at sprouts, you must have gawped with joy
at that strange white till your face got fixed that way.

JUMP-CUTS

As if Hopper had travelled in time to Glencoe —
the wall orange with sun, the two gilt mirrors
and Brenda's son in his Adidas shellsuit looking on

from his stool as out of your reticent back
your mum's head like a second head emerges
to make small talk with his mum's baby bump.

None of these for me, I'm not a real person
you'd said as we leafed through the airbrushed snaps
splayed across the varnish like a conjuror's cards.

～

The trick is to look dreamy but not orgasmic
as nubile fingers knead shampoo through my hair;
as licks of lather are towelled off my brow

I squint up at the ceiling with wild surmise
like some metrosexual Rocky Balboa,
then rise from my corner for the last round

of the Prozac rope-a-dope — withdrawal
symptoms, that five-week half-life
has me glitching up as I'm offered tea.

～

The scene kids cover one eye, or both.
I'd say Gabrielle did it better back in the 90s
but of course she had a ptosis. The nineties,
back when the slogan from *Generation X*

153

said HAIR IS YOUR DOCUMENT. You show me
Beyoncé's weave flamed by her wind machine,

reality TV: a stylist with no signature cut
is pressured to revamp his ailing salon.
Bullying then transformation; a familiar format.

RECESSION

Down an iron spiral staircase like a trilobite,
remembering aggrieved suits at the bar,
past shanties painted gaily, fooling no one
we arrive in the dishevelment of our aspirations

at the square of this ghost town where the dust
comes at you breast-high, like the swimming pool
one's back yard used to boast, a blue stone
of the finest water. The built landscape

in our heads could not, after all, be numbered
reliably as our hairs; lucky for some,
the automatic elegance of phrasing
a salary in the low six figures will transmit

to its blasé dependants, blessed with a sense
that any room they enter is all ears
tuned in to their nice discriminations . . .
A boho hobo tweets his blues up the stairwell.

DOT DOT DOT

After dinner we see a fingerprint
lifted, germ-luminous, off the guilty surface;
another leaps from the victim's thigh
like the bright bands of a bee
and fairly zooms at the eye, as if saying
the wackos were right, steel wouldn't melt

at that temperature, and yes, everyone hates you . . .
That night, I dream an avenue of limes
at dusk, odorous, wondering
what exactly it is I'm advertising
before I realise I can't know exactly
how each leaf looks on each tree—

I might as well number the telogen hairs
responsible for our flooding shower,
the bezoars of our couplehood
one may only lift from the plughole
with a beckoning finger, as if trying
for the fabled G-spot . . .

SOPHIE ROBINSON

◇ ◇ ◇

Sophie Robinson was born in 1985. She has an MA in Poetic Practice, and is currently completing a practice-based PhD in Queer Phenomenology and Contemporary Poetry at Royal Holloway. Her first book, a, came out from Les Figues press in 2009. Her work has been included in several anthologies including *Infinite Difference: Other Poetries by Women in the UK* (Shearsman 2010), *Voice Recognition* (Bloodaxe, 2009) and *The Reality Street Book of Sonnets* (Reality Street 2008). In January 2011, she was appointed as poet in residence at the V&A Museum.

FLESH LEGGINGS

A persuasive blackness of spirit touches
You, & I do not have the answer you
Feel you deserve. Your olive oil stomach
Is calling out for the thrill of lips, &
Your hurt curls are enshrined in cotton.
Small and puffy by the door, a backless
Vibration falls amongst us, a low-flowered
Anger. You hold out your palms of feel the
Chesty pulses, and soon it creeps in you,
Harping over and over the hands and

Cities. The loving diagnosis of
Your hip shot from grace —a stapler greeted
By skin, broke, fell to earth like a gazelle.

WINDED BY LOVE

And what hurt her damp hand touched with
Her nose in her arm—
Her cut knees waste away below her
Those beyond tones, with sore-belted lips
Flower that last hip, drown hard in rebuke
Oily fingers in a jar, a legging-lover squatting
In the low-ribbed land, gingerly gurning towards
A peekaboo crotch vibrating against a useless
Void of understanding, the owl's head hung
At the sight of people going broken, let
My tape dispenser run long against my
Starred earlobe—you are a held place &
Your palms beg me not to gaze—
Swollen like dogs we will live forever
In this mess—malachite bellies held proud
And bare

ANIMAL HOSPITAL

Some times like sin sugar that broke that crashes
Bruise of rib like rip off cloth and let salt
Winds scathe in eye in face I am sandy,
Long for ocean grind—but shy, but shy—"I
Don't owe you any money don't have to
Show you all my things"—just live, okay? "Cause
All our money is etch-a-sketch, and I
Think too often about the forward times
When our things are out and old on the street,

When we are out of time, stink, are the laughed
At lucky ones or, worse, screaming in two
Different hospitals, species strangers,
Unknown/unknowing.

                              This is the ailing
Of peace, the rearrangement of passion.
We do not kiss but strum ourselves apart.
The sun has its sins, the heart its heavy.
This poem should be longer, and more careful.
Give me time.

from S H E !

do you in all my emptiness feel me
felt like dollies?   I wish now to tie my
self inside your strange and static chest. Coins
astonish me, sitting yellowish and
relenting as ornaments worn around
your neck. You have the most benevolent
hips this side of god. I would eat the pole
which holds your constellation steady in
a second, wolfishly.

                              ∾

the woofs of distant dogs waft overhead. Shall
we do shots? Nitty gritty lo and hi
jive strewn across the length of the bar.
spunky tinctures spew their way into us.
grab my glad rags and realize I am
serious. This kiss is elixir and
undermines the minor players struck
by chairs or friends, juicing the youth
from this room in which we root our meat,
the queasy teddy of our affection.

                              ∾

state separation, stigma hid
in eely illusion of pink
glister, expleting shades of ripe
lies to fatten the gape, *suffer*
this: this future sutures you in
to where the limit is squeamish,
some scrappy snarl of modish
necessity basting us
in only to roast us later,
juicy and spurting to the last:
what does it mean: the decency
of voices? Make anger hash from
well-bred kleptos of humanity.

CHARLOTTE RUNCIE

◊ ◊ ◊

Charlotte Runcie shares her time between Edinburgh and London, and read English at Cambridge University. She is co-editor of *Pomegranate* poetry ezine and has had work published in various magazines. Her pamphlet *Seventeen Horse Skeletons* was part of the tall-lighthouse Pilot series. She was a Foyle Young Poet of the Year in 2006 and won first prize in the Christopher Tower Poetry Prizes in 2007.

STAYING IN

I watch the city shrug its clothes back on.
An appaloosa spatter gathers scent
that hits the brain the way it hits a lawn:
it quenches, hard as mint. I think it meant
to come inside, but only leaves a note
in droplets on the door; at Hogmanay
it settles in the lungs and in the throat
and whispers too a hush of seaside spray
that sweeps below the ribs and keeps its snow
flakes back from hopeful tongues. I'm breathing when
the rainsmell pours my throat a dram, and so
I open up the window wider, stand again

here in our cloud and wincing, hats and boots,
a pearlish weeping reaching for the roots.

THE SEVENTH WINTER

Yes,
we've lost that many men to avalanche.
By summer we mourned every hour of sunlight
we had given to the north.

In autumntime we saved up salt
to melt away our murderer as if he were a slug,
before he pushed his one white foot
into our house. In January
he took a taste and licked his lips
and moved a little closer.

My sister planted seventeen bare birch trees
in a line behind our house,
a sacrifice to snowdrifts.

I can see them from our kitchen window.
They are seventeen horse skeletons,
their backs against the wind.
They know their spines will break for us,
and in the storms
I feel them shivering.

This is how it is with us.
We hold back snow with bones.

POPE, TELESCOPE

He smoothes his hands over its hips
and pulls its eye to rest against his own,
zooms into the dark to study fireflakes
strung up and blizzarding
across the dome of atmosphere.
Psalms and intercessions drift
in universal rafters, with Sunday smoke
from mouths, and lungs
broadcasting into black.

As he focuses the glass into the distance,
it doesn't seem to matter if
the star above the stable
was really only Jupiter,
bending closer just to see the fuss;

he means to keep an eye out for
his echoes bouncing off the asteroids,
in case an eardrum reaches up to catch
and beats a sacred cadence back.

Each night he sieves the cosmos through his sinuses
and scans the skies for codes, or explanations—
come morning, as the sun brights out the blueprint
he swings a fiery meteor
to wash the earth in outer space.

FUR

In the lounge she wore a stole
of long albino eyelashes
pulled loose and bound,
threaded in a winter knit.
Her faint neck rose
from porcupine icicles, a

stiff vogue brush of fishbones.

She unwound it in the powder room,
uncovering bare alcoves
around her collarbone, exposing
something of the tundra,
her muscles wrapped in wide white plains.

At the door I clothe her again
in other creatures' skin.
Shivering I press myself
to chalky bones and gauze,
the fabric of her cheek,
inhaling fox fur,
her breathing in my hair a ghost.

IN MY POCKET

"My heart is in my
pocket, it is Poems by Pierre Reverdy."
—Frank O'Hara, A Step Away From Them

"Pikachu, I choose you!"
—Pokémon

Electric fighting bug,
water grass and fire.
Six balled-up monsters
slung around my hips.

For now they must be fruit:
I palm one, feel the pores
and bowl, and blinking down
just when it splits

I splinter into anime.
A heart is shared in six:
a team of hearts in red-and-white
in jeans, my hand and pack,

caught systems of defense
once wild. Imagination loves,
jack-in-the-boxes fighting
from a pen made out of oranges.

ASHNA SARKAR

◊ ◊ ◊

Ashna Sarkar was born in 1992 in North London. She is currently an undergraduate at University College London where she is studying English Literature. Her poems have been featured in *City State: The New London Poetry* (Penned in the Margins, 2009), and she was one of the Foyle Young Poets of the Year in 2009.

HEARTBEAT

Trawlerman is the most southerly chippie in North Weezy
to do chips with onion gravy.
So I'm not surprised when Turnbull suggests we meet here
to point out my first mistake. *"Wrong side of the Calder,"*
he says of the Rochdale boy who stole a Topshop blazer and
The Horrors' new EP upon breakup.
As for the Chelsea Trustafarian; *"any boy can hothouse weed
under UV, but it takes a real man to work an allotment."*
The organic veg box delivered each week did not count.

He sighs through my catalogue of Sloanes, Vice bloggers,
weedgies, thrift whores and Welsh funky house enthusiasts.
I blunder through all the wrong bits of Britain.

When he hears of an honest to God Barnsley FC supporting
and Hovis eating son-of-Yorkshire chased away,
he pauses
on a mouthful of skate.
"Perhaps you talk too much love, when a clip round t'ear would do."

CARRY ON CUTTING

The son-in-law was a regular specimen.
Anatomically correct;
finger tip to tip measuring a middle height,
 a normal sort of pendulum
to tick away mechanical bedtime appointments.

To think those painfully average hands
would cart off her most treasured work.
Her own marriage? Red in tooth and claw.
John was like the conjoined tangle of his house;
the fashionable face of Leicester Square knocked through
to the dissecting rooms of Castle Street, where pale faces
of the poor and deformed stare back from green jars.

When he brought back the bones of an Irish Giant,
Anne wished her daughter could marry a man like that.
To be loved by his big flat hands, to swing on his shoulders
while his step spans three shires toward home.

THE NEW VINCE

"That's the new me!" Vince sings,
"That kid shows real potential."
Tim's already bedding the Pride of Finchley.
His old man? Never a skinny jean donned in his puff.

166

"That kid shows real potential."
Vince always said his own folks had no music in them;
his old man? Never a skinny jean donned in his puff,
only the bass line beat of Vinnie's shoes on the driveway.

Vince always said his own folks had no music in them.
Tim's already bedding the Pride of Finchley.
Only the bass line beat of Vinnie's shoes on the driveway;
"That's the new me," Vince sings.

SETTING SUN

Southgate's own sticky dream by the Punto-ful
—edible dresses, creamy arms and legs made jelly by Stoli
and a white label sub-bass shudder. We pull up against a red light;
you try to look to the next-door Micra as though you're sleeping
with at least two of us.

Streetlamp licks shift and slide over chipped paintwork, the
colour changing like evening and we howl as the sky plunges from plum
to blueberry. You push your foot into carpet, your future brightens, we
Snarl up Shoreditch High Street. This could be our last shout.

In a few weeks, you'll picnic on
lawns hushed like libraries, rich with Jenny's spilled Cava, books,
and sniff that Tarquin missed. You'll cough up the aitches and glottal
stops swallowed last summer. You'll put the Punto on eBay
and start cycling.

Until then, one delicious July, the best since we learnt how to drink, you say.
We'll gorge ourselves on friendship while we can. A wobble of wheel spin
has you shook. We scream; we want to go faster
and you, you realise you're better off

walking.

WILLIAM SEARLE

◊ ◊ ◊

William Searle was born in Dorset in 1987 and grew up in the New Forest. He studied English at Royal Holloway, then took an MA in Creative Writing. He received an AHRC Studentship award to do a PhD in Creative Writing, supervised by Sir Andrew Motion and is living in Snowdonia, North Wales.

CONSIDER THIS

Here we have no shotguns, no shacks to burn,
rebuild, re-burn, no iron coyotes haunting
the bayou, toughened tornadoes brandishing
lightning. There, you can break what you want.

Here is mirror-crisp. I breathe fragile frost-
shocked air. Innocent vandal, give me back
my glass goblet of rain decorated with
delicate herons, slow bolts from the blue,

like porcelain Gods sluggish over the sullen,
widespread face of the deep. Even our horses
are mild-thighed. Leeches make fine black
crystal bracelets. The sun is often lost in a

mayhem of cloud. This is my makeshift Eden.
I re-make it like pottery with secret tools
every dawn before you've finished dreaming,
but it shatters into a irretrievable mosaic

of the moon by the merest thought of you.
You must change your tact if you wish to be
welcome here. Don't let this turn into a fiasco.
Just say, say that I have tried and tried again.

THE DAIMON

The bonfire purred and wagged.
Ash veils purled, pillowed, flaked
blossom-like into plumes, touch-
papers, brocades, svelte pot pourri.

An aerosol tossed in from darkness
sent up punctual whumphs, ruining
orders of fire colour into a knee-high
vortex of black-ash, irking embers
back into flame, scoffing Guy Fawkes,

with his ball-in-sock head crowned
in Catherine wheels, —he fizzed. But
what caught my eye was a vague man,
sidestepping behind our garden's

shrub-border, gnawing his top lip,
clapping with the backs of his hands,
going still to gasp in the night air,
shudder rigid, then point fiercely at me.

A NOCTURNAL PACT

Grass munched peppered with earwigs,
hoverflies that tremored amazed us more
than hawks tethered to God's hand of blue.

Brothers dream of being brothers again
where the paint-faded fence met the house
and in that corner, kneeled in nettle and dock-leaves,

you stepped up onto my back, hauled yourself over
then thumped down upon the neighbour's weird arena.
Strange, unforgiving you returned after time,

slinked away into obscurity with bruised shins,
starving stomach and asthmatic lungs.
I hear your screaming coda of growing-pains

from where you must of vanished to-
closer than breath, further off than I can imagine.
I stand where cobwebs shake and ivy grips a brick.

A VISIT

Black-out in Bateley Mill.
My Grandfather, to work
in the dark, worked in
the dark, to home in the dark,

slouched during a break
over a coarse plywood
desk, glowed in the dark
because of his flour-dusted

apron, forearms and face,
poised his head owl-slow

in position to hold his breath,
factory lights dimmed alarmingly

distant as stars, rats fidgeted
in the pipes. No wonder then,
after my Mother seeing him
like that, went through a phase

of running from the moon.

COLETTE SENSIER

◇ ◇ ◇

Colette Sensier was born in Brighton in 1988 and grew up in Sussex. She studied English at King's College, Cambridge, and is currently living in London. She has been a first-prize winner of the Foyle's, Tower and Peterloo young poets' competitions, and was featured in the anthology *Poetry South-East 2010* and the Oxfam young poets' DVD anthology *Asking a Shadow to Dance*.

TOOTHLESSNESS

Perhaps the breast was disappeared too quickly,
anyway, I stayed orally fixated, my fingers never
out of my mouth. Each tooth was touched
a hundred times a day, sprung soldiers,

each one weak. I had dreams I'd lose my teeth.
Tar beasties, sucked down, swirled
inside my mouth's rough darkness, harsh
as orange peel—I dreamed of a kiss so vast

that we'd fuse like fish, enter the prehistory of kisses,
tongues larger than night or water—my husband,

we grew to be elderly. Each yellow peg
fell into our shared sink, the blood palpable taste,

moist time. Now, mouth wet as pulp or bog,
the tongue lives alone—save you—pressing down
sometimes in the darkness, beneath my touch.
Still alive, my mouth—sometimes I think I hear it moan.

ORPHEUS

I

After I'd hustled, somehow, my way through overdrafts and overtime, goat-
   sitting,
busking on street corners—I drew quite a crows—into the trans-
   continental-ticket-bracket,
packed my handbooks and mosquito nets, boarded at the Styx and sung the
   long
ripped song of the aeroplane, a birdcall lost in chasing cloud, I landed slap-
   bang in the middle

of Mahebourg Market, Mauritius: the place I'd hoped to seek her out, my other
   half,
my home; the wandering, trapped part of my soul I'd been promised I could
   always return to.
I staggered when I got there though, under the weight of clatter and the
   strange stray dogs
and white wolves of waves stroking the surfaces of a landscape burnt too hot
   for me.

And I despaired: the thing that I most wanted nowhere to be found among
the t-shirts imported from Japan, the clack of boules, the bang of stacked
   chapatti pans,
and behind the stalls, the gasp of local magicians astonished at themselves
and all they had to offer. Was that her eye in the eye of a fat round fish

173

flapping at the top of a silvery pile, sounding the echo of a sunbeam?
Was that her body turning in the pink jewelled sari held up for admiration,
moving like mobile hair or flayed skin? The imam called over my head,
remember to submit. The church bells told me, *come back to God*. Salt scent
     whispered

behind lashes and fingernails, weaving across the veins at my wrists. My lute
     bumped
against the suddenly wrong skin of my thigh, a skin too pale and too loosely
     held to bone,
as I dodged from toe to toe and string to string around the docks, never fast
     enough
to catch a single sincere note; as policemen with their bushed moustaches,

their blue shirts and shaded eyes watched me like deaf spirits, separated
     tourists
I saw who dared to kiss. *Is this, sir, what you're looking for? Peek quickly or*
they'll kick me out, he opened up the long flat hook of his grey suitcase, the lid
     swung open
like the stone before a tomb . . .

II

     Many words have been offered to or given me:
     Greek or Turkish? Italiano, Espagnol? There's no way
     you're not Israeli or *Where was your mother from?*
     At most, *You have the island look. Caribbean?*
     but here they speak to me in Kreol, watch me

     as I walk down the street—until I answer and,
     as always, disappoint: my staccato English
     failed again. So my mouth and limbs stay folded up.
     I watch my grandparents instead
     as they lie on tender beaches, remembering;

     or else I watch the people as they move
     from one small spot to the next. Their faces
     are heavy in the shade, reflecting,
     like thick glass tilted towards the sun,
     nothing but the island's hot light. Nothing of me.

It's not many human creatures who — with skin
living and flexible working over solid limbs
full of dry, shining, salted bone,
a purple pumping heart, kidneys and lungs —
will know the feeling of complete immersion,
a journey to another land behind a wall of salt
and glass and water. It's not many who cross
that floating river, spitting pomegranate seeds,
and live to tell the tale.

But when you dove off that ledge or throne of rock
and felt the water popping in your ears,
scouring your throat to take what it discovered there,
peeling that last layer of skin around your lips,
you knew you had become mankind, and knew
what you had found — a story that would save us all,
the hint of an ending in eighteen feet of water,
a glimpse of Eurydice.

And then the tight space in your chest denied
further investigation, the last page. You swam,
your eyes stinging too freely to look back,
the frog-kicks of your legs making their own
ripples, you stood a wet mess on the slippery surface,
your body newly yours, the laughing children
emerging from the dawn around you
to jump again and again
without a second thought.

EVOLUTION

First, the round cheek of the taut stomach,
navel an ear or blowhole, listening out
for signals from the curved inverted globe.
Then the bones, once out, moulding their sphere.

The halfway house retreats. Darkened eyelashes
frame new eyes; the layer of thin dried yoghurt
flakes away, coarse hair falls from his cheeks
in the slow move from prehistory to now,

a gill-less creature. Or, as things would go for me:
the face smoothes itself out as I recline, Madonna
of the incidental, waiting for the roots of things
to become apparent. Guileless, I listen to lost notes,

the silent progress of the gut-shot features
swimming back to their original element.

WARSAN SHIRE

◊ ◊ ◊

Warsan Shire is a Somali writer born in Nairobi in 1988. She is an artistic activist with a degree in Creative Writing. Her poetry has been translated into Italian, Spanish and Portuguese. Her pamphlet *Teaching Mother How To Give Birth* is from Flipped Eye.

UGLY

Your daughter is ugly.
She knows loss intimately,
carries whole cities in her belly.

As a child, relatives wouldn't hold her.
She was splintered wood and sea water.
They said she reminded them of the war.

On her fifteenth birthday you taught her
how to tie her hair like rope
and smoke it over burning frankincense.

You made her gargle rosewater
and while she coughed, said

macaanto girls like you shouldn't smell
of lonely or empty.

You are her mother.
Why did you not warn her,
hold her like a rotting boat
and tell her that men will not love her
if she is covered in continents,
if her teeth are small colonies,
if her stomach is an island
if her thighs are borders?

What man wants to lay down
and watch the world burn
in his bedroom?

Your daughter's face is a small riot,
her hands are a civil war,
a refugee camp behind each ear,
a body littered with ugly things

but God,
doesn't she wear
the world well.

THINGS WE HAD LOST IN THE SUMMER

I

The summer my cousins return from Nairobi,
we sit in a circle by the oak tree in my aunt's garden
and they look older. Amel's hardened nipples push through
the paisley of her blouse, minarets calling men to worship.

When they left, I was twelve years old and swollen

178

with the heat of waiting. We hugged at the departure gate,
waifs with bird chests clinking like wood, boyish,
long skirted figurines waiting to grow

intoour hunger. My mother uses her quiet voice
on the phone:
   Are they all okay? Are they healing well?
She doesn't want my father to overhear.

II

Juwariyah, my age, leans in and whispers,
I've started my period. Her hair is in my mouth when
I try to move in closer—*how does it feel?*

She turns to her sisters and a laugh that is not hers
stretches from her body like a moan.
She is more beautiful than I can remember.

One of them pushes my open knees closed.
Sit like a girl. I finger the hole in my shorts,
shame warming my skin.

In the car, my mother stares at me through the
rear view mirror, the leather sticks to the back of my
thighs. I open my legs like a well oiled door,

daring her to look at me and give me
what I had not lost; a name.

MAYMUUN'S MOUTH

Maymuun lost her accent with
the help of her local Community College.
Most evenings she calls me long distance
to discuss the pros and cons

of heating molasses in the microwave
to remove body hair. Her new voice

is sophisticated. She has taken to dancing
in front of strangers. She lives next door
to a Dominican who speaks to her in Spanish
whenever they pass each other in hallways.
I know she smiles at him, front teeth stained
from the fluoride in the water back home.
She's experiencing new things. We understand.

We've received the photos of her standing
by a bridge, the baby hair she'd hated all her life
slicked down like ravines. Last week
her answering machine picked up.
I imagined her hoisted by the waist,
wearing stockings, learning to kiss
with her new tongue.

BEAUTY

My older sister soaps between her legs, her hair
a prayer of curls. When she was my age, she stole
the neighbour's husband, burnt his name into her skin.
For weeks she smelt of cheap perfume and dying flesh.

It's 4 a.m. and she winks at me, bending over the sink,
her small breasts bruised from sucking,
she smiles, pops her gum before saying —
boys are haram, don't ever forget that.

Some nights I hear her in her room screaming.
We play Surah al-Baqarah to drown her out.
Anything that leaves her mouth sounds like sex.
Our mother has banned her from saying God's name.

LAVINIA SINGER

◇ ◇ ◇

Lavinia Singer was born in London in 1988. She studied English at the University of Oxford, where she won the Newdigate Prize in 2010. Lavinia is currently the intern at *Poetry Review* and starts a Masters in Creative Writing at Royal Holloway in 2011.

THE MAPMAKER'S DAUGHTER

When the door is shut, I know He's at work.
Creating worlds by the flow of a pen tip—
I used to think He was a god, crafting
with quadrant and accurate vernier.
In seven days separating water from land,
A straining Newton with compasses clutched
dextrously mapping Particles of Light.

When the electricity blared its last,
He took to lighting candle stubs, the flames
licking the ink so the colours blinked like stained glass.
Toffee shores glowed like half moons, round
with sand tumbling like uncountable kisses.

From coast to peninsula, each scrub and each dab
plotted a country, a nation, a home.

When bored in the house and Him locked away
I'd be content with an old mottled print
scouted out at a car boot sale,
amid chipped tea cup and watering can.
A *mappus mundi*, Dad said. No ordinary map!
Its circles and symbols resembled a code,
and the land it outlaid was like none I had known.

When science and story were one, and
the globe some plump orb of possibility,
where cave-dwelling giants mixed with dog-headed men,
dwarves riding on crocodiles, and charmers of snakes.
I'd stare at those figures holding their heads
like swollen shopping bags, and little folk
gathering silk worms by the Tree of Life.

When the forests here went, I missed the green
of Dad's work. Colour of the kind that sits
in front of your face, sucking your eyeballs.
The white of the icebergs too, melted away.
His parchment now looks like something deceased,
brown like tough skin with odd cities freckled,
rivers of wrinkles and washed stains of blue.

O the blue!

Now oceans rise and Neptune conquers all,
The tide a hiccup choking up upon shore.
Nothing can stop the waves, as they soar—
stealing strips of terrain, smashing houses and shops.
Now all that Dad's map shows are disparate islands,
bobbing bits of broken turf, continents cracked.
The monsters have gone now, and many men too.

Now all Dad needs is tins of cyan,
turquoise and teal and ultramarine,
the blues of midnight, lavender and sky.

And me? I look at my old print now
and an old Ordnance Survey of his.
They both show a world I can barely believe.
A world that was marvellous.
A world that was good.

NOVEMBER

The evening comes much quicker now,
but has threatened us all day.
Each yew tree is half cloaked
by shadow, the colour of mud.

The cold is felt inside deep socks,
sweaters, crept beneath the threads
to lie down like a lifeless sparrow.
Ice at the fingertips.

The leaves have drooped,
now rot, will freeze.
The willow clings to its adornments,
and hot white stars still sear.

THE ANCHORITE

Penance, poverty, a life of prayer
withdrawn, world-starved, but clean and pure in God.
When left to softly waste, limbs become stone
cold inside the cell and Time reverses.
Her body shrinks and tongue forgets its words.
Is this a Woman with her scooped-out chest,
her skull shaved? No scarlet stain will grace
the rag that sits unknown between her thighs.
No fingertip of Man will trace her form

to smooth the jut of ribs—just spotless light
pressing through the pane to greet her skin.

INTERNAL MEMORANDUM

i.m. *John Ddungu*
i.m. *Tobias Rundle*

We found them sitting there like little souls,
slips of paper marked carefully with ink,
fluttering whitely in our pigeonholes.
Curious, I skim read till the room shrinks—

and just like that a day falls apart,
scattering its hours and minutes like
tired blossoms that sink, becoming part
of the wind; a surrender. I felt sick

when the ambulance came. Someone
whistling is a slap in the face. It's
a movie where every character is dumb:
gormless in a horror of nonsense . . .

Now there's a flag; it shrugs a bit
in the quad. We, too, shrug, and move,
making our bodies, little systems, fit
in rooms, shaping sounds with our mouths

as I think we used to. Forgetting the use of them;
a lot is missing. Even a hug seems
empty at the centre, ever since that memo.
College lies dipped in daydream.

But Oxford strides on through the term,
and so we strive to keep up close,
dust off our knees, begin to learn.
Without hurry, the old purpose

returns, and so do friends I'd missed.
Like when a chain loses one of its links,
the others press tight together round the wrist.
Our lives beat on, close-knit, in sync.

So the seasons speed right on through December
from blossom to snowflakes, changes of weather,
but the internal memorandum is still there:
Inside, we will, we must, remember.

ADHAM SMART

◊ ◊ ◊

Adham Smart was born in Cambridge in 1992 and grew up in Cairo and London. He won the Foyle Young Poets of the Year Awards in 2006, 2008 and 2009. He was commended in the *Mimesis* digital chapbook competition 2008, and had writing in *The Cadaverine Anthology* (Cadaverine Magazine, 2009), *Obakarama* (Sidekick Books, 2009) and *Korsakoff's Paper Chain* (Sidekick Books, 2010). He is one of the editors of *Pomegranate* ezine for younger poets. He is currently studying Georgian and Linguistics at SOAS.

THE NEW MECHANICS

For years I dreamt in black and white,
Greek letters and explosions, the smallest pieces
of shape and weight dancing through the dark.
I lost months of sleep, yet no-one
ever asked me how I had slept. Wrapped in dripping sheets,
I wrestled nightly with the elements, a torment of theories
that broke, wave-like, on a moonlit beach.

That was me. I spent my youth fixing the perfect atom
with stiffened fingers, drawing cold breaths,
filling my lungs with chalk.

PUMPKIN HEART BOY

A lovester after his own fashion, he took her
hand and held it in his. Oh, was he a wonder-
kid, his hair in tufts and sweeping waves
like dolphins surfacing in a line. Golden-eyed,
he licked her lips with hand on thigh,
and stroked that pillar of bone and skin,
told her that she was more than meat to him.
His pumpkin heart, more than a muscle,
drummed and drummed and drummed and
drummed the boy and girl into the heat
of being loved and not being meat.
A sweetened lifting of his senses
drove to dreams of burning clouds. It was
the longest time they'd felt the breath
of this pumpkin life, that never-death.

O, OPENMOUTHED, YOU ARE
ONE OF US

We saw you walking in with frightened steps.
You were blind to candled faces,
shrouded but shining, glowing
at your side. You did not know

the way back and you could not see
what you approached, child, you did not
understand. We can teach you everything
you do not know. Ah, Child, we saw you shining in,

wings dazzling and eyes declaring: "I am not a burning candle."
Our hands are clean, our beards are black, our vision
is sharp, yet we are blind, O, we are blind, but surely
we saw you walking in.

Come and lick our bones clean of sin,
read for us the writing on the stone. We read
but do not understand. We are a splintered island
and surely you are glowing, Child. Wash our faces

with your tongue, take us far from this city
where they shroud us in black and push our voices
down below, where we are blind to shining candles
and open wings, where all we have are whispered
emergencies and we blindly fight what we do not
understand, Child, take us in a gasp of burning
air, the kind we all know best, Child, do not
hesitate, we all are waiting, and we can see
you walking weepingly away, but there
is nothing that can frighten you now
for we have conquered your body
and our mark is on your skin
and underneath it in the
places that you do not
know but that we
surely do—

and now be one of us. Ah, Child,
we saw you walking in with frightened steps.
O, Openmouthed, you are one of us!
We saw you walking in.

MARTHA SPRACKLAND

◊　◊　◊

Martha Sprackland was born in 1988, and grew up in Merseyside. After two years as a language teacher in Madrid, she moved back to the UK to read English Literature and Creative Writing at Lancaster University. This year she begins an MA in English Literary Studies. She was twice a Foyle Young Poet and co-edits *Cake* Magazine.

PLATE

You held it to yourself one night
clasped the cold white china
against your breast like a shield
suds stained dark your blue shirt
like the army march of lichen.
Stood still beside the deep sea sink
you curled your hands around the edge
felt the soft ecstatic curve
the rolling drips from the glaze
locked tight like icicles
caught at the thaw.
I heard you in the kitchen
laughing at the hectic tearing

of rubber gloves from your hands
to grasp the cold surface
the joy of tasting something solid,
the absolute sweetness of material.

SECOND BODY

Sometimes in the mirror the one body blurs
slips its grasp on time
and space, and liberates a second body
prismatic, like the shadows cast by stage lights.

There's a bigger something in there,
some tangential woman
with rounded camber
silvered with glacier tracks.
A body whose breasts are drops of rain.

When someone else touches her
she's smooth like a fastened acorn,
but in the tropics of the shower
her own four hands recall
the budding and contracting
the swell and sprout and
the cut-off which split,
by parthenogenesis,
one human woman into two.

The shadow-body lingers in the steam
like the delay on a bad tape,
or drunken double vision,
the vertigo at the brink of the anaesthesia.

The awakening, though, she remembers.
A first glimpse in a passing mirror
to the other woman's other body,

newly arrived, and
her voice perpetual as a stuck record
too late, vowing
never, never to let it go.

THE GOLD

In her eighth month with me she was enormous.
I've sorted through the pictures —
she's smiling, both palms flat against her bump
as if offering it up to the camera in my father's hands.

No wedding ring on
because of the swollen fingers —
the plain gold band had been cutting in
and as they walked together down the village
she was working and twisting at it until
with a sudden gathering of strength it had flown
winking sunlight back at them as
they watched the curve of its trajectory
its landing, its wobble as it rolled
drunkenly, towards the mouth of the drain.

I can imagine my father leaping into action
the open front of his shirt streaming back as
in the nick of time he gets there
stamps down hard on the lip of the grate
and they both fall about.

I wear it now, sometimes
on a chain fed through
the flattened, doubled gold.
Not smooth any more
the gleam from the bottom of the prospector's pan,
this golden thing I've sifted out and salvaged.

TIME CAPSULE

Peeling back a plane of wallpaper
you turned to me, elated
and I felt the anarchic satisfaction of skinning.
I swung a graft of the stuff up
the dust eddying
the edges leaving themselves behind.

There is pleasure, too
in the fiddly lap at the light switch
or when the paper slips its ply
and leaves behind a clean, white layer
the shape of a continent on a map.

Sometimes there have been marks
functional, mechanical
24xr / elec.
the red chalk workings of plumber
builder, electrician.

Rarer still
the scrawl in biro
like the time we sloughed the hall
uncovering two names and a date
decades old.

While you pasted a fresh strip
I lingered at the wall
sure of their fingerprints in the plaster
of voices, laughter.

ELOISE STONBOROUGH

◊ ◊ ◊

Eloise Stonborough was born in London in 1988. She studied English Literature at St Edmund Hall, Oxford where she won the Graham Midgley Prize for poetry and where she was also Secretary of the Oxford Poetry Society. She has recently completed a Master's degree in English, also at St Edmund Hall, and is beginning a DPhil at Balliol College, Oxford where she will be working on the connections between form and poetic personality in twentieth century poetry.

FUGUE STATE

I have dreamt of screen doors opening
onto long peculiar paths, still wild
or close enough in this slow
ancestral light, and drawing in
my skirts to walk barefoot on the grass;
skin so tender it bruised
at every step. I couldn't say more,
not while the wind fills the blinds
and the pigeons rage, but sometimes
it comes back to me as I trail the end
of my cigarette against its echo
and stare at my ghost in the glass.

There is nothing so marvelled here
among the resting armies of signs
and empty gates; nothing to mask
how I drift further into the deep
sly arc of evening and lose
my feeling for the world, my fires
burning on notebooks. I haven't spoken
in days, it seems, or weeks,
and I am hounded by my silence
following me everywhere, snagging
on parked cars like a petulant shadow,
catching my breath as I sleep.

THE PHARAOH'S EMBALMERS

The embalmers knew the brain for what it is:
the upstart ancestor of phlegm; a distraction
from their tidy catalogue of flesh. Each organ
in its jar protected by a tiny clay-faced god,
quantifiable in their order: the stomach,
for its hunger, guarded by the jackal;
the curving intestines hovered over
by a falcon; the lungs' breath clouding
in the throat of the wide-jawed baboon;
and the liver, the last, most human organ,
topped with a man's face, dark as blood.

The brain has no place, tugged out through
the nose and thrown to the dusty kittens
crowding the door of the high temple.
In this canopic peace there is no room
to unpick its madman scrawls, puzzle out
the smooth grey ciphers of its knots,
better to leave that to the earth. The afterlife
demands only one organ as you enter
to be weighed against the ghost of flight
imprinted on a feather, so they leave the heart
as witness in the safest cage a body knows.

THE MERCY GLASS

I

Most days, lust is enough to fatten the cheeks
of a dreary afternoon: a sudden sting from a wasp
caught dozing in the cuffs of a mothballed coat.

The innocent call this temptation, as if it flickered
on the soul's backwaters like ghost lights,
as if it waited to lure the unwary to their deaths.

But lust breeds in the absence of softer pleasures,
its litters mewling through an empty gut,
their tiny mouths scarlet and filled with knives.

II

Will they come to the cuckold's house or mine,
with a little rough music for the wastrel heart?

I am not the girl for whom my mother kept
her mother's pearls, the kind of girl

who leaves before the postman. How easily
admission absolves the bastard from remorse.

III

We are devoted to narrowing the margins
of loss, working out a smaller toll of mercies
as if allowing a moment to swell into its own
painful honesty would be another failure,

a testament to our imperfect arrogance,
carved out of chipboard and tarnished glass,
impervious to the violent longings of a self
that seeks always to be worlds above reproach.

Forgive me. I am thrown to my knees
in the frozen posture of the unaccustomed supplicant
tracing the latticework on the confessional,
searching for mercy. It will never come.

CHAOS

Why are we, born in the rubble of an old order,
shocked by the body's drift to fervour?

The question is no longer that of living, but how
to keep lost comforts purring through the static

of a time (and we count it minute by minute) that offers
little more than the hum of libraries

fading into obsolescence. Watch the schoolyards
scream into the street, spilling their lives

as if they grew unnumbered in the eaves
of their whispered attic haunts. Perhaps they do,

we are not privy to the casual violence
of our children's minds. It is a new game,

this playing the electric down the backs of our skin,
and how can we be sure that our presence

isn't twisting the world into new miseries;
its lightning flickering in a spinning coin,

demanding choice when all we crave is freedom.

EMILY TESH

◊ ◊ ◊

Emily Tesh was born in London in 1988. She studied Classics at Trinity College, Cambridge, where she won prizes for original verse and verse translation, and is currently a graduate student at the University of Chicago after being awarded an exchange studentship for her creative writing. She was a winner of the Foyle Young Poets of the Year award in 2006, and is a member of the editorial team for the youth poetry zine *Pomegranate*.

AT SEA

I have seen the water taking you.
I have seen the deep green northern thunder
crashing over you, Atlantic hunger
swallowing the towers and the streets,
swallowing the leafy cool retreats
where we two kissed beneath the willow trees.

Stir up ashy foam and black and blue,
and call the ancient serpents and the sharks;
Leviathan will circle in the dark.
Since you have brought my borrowed kingdom down,

I hope you die. I hope, I hope you drown.
I hope the current kisses like the breeze.

(DONA NOBIS PACEM)

Oh god, it feels so strange to love a place
thoughtlessly, to love your booted feet
because the snow is on them, to sense grace

bleeding through the still and snowsoft air
above the spiky roofs of empty chapels
and hunger to drag God away from there

to stand out in the holy streets and cry
havoc over fallen towers, change
beneath an arched unseen uncareful sky.

THREE SONNETS FOR A GIRL

I.

In low-lit clubs, the costume jewellery sparkled
heartless, with the purple drained like grapeskin
just after wine is pressed. Your hair was dark
and red by turns. (The dye was seeping in
last week, with orange stripes like tangerines
unpeeling in the smoke.) I saw you smile
around the tips of fags. Now when I dream
you burn like shots. You linger on a while.

Tell me what to do now, smudge my eyes
with streaks of paint like yours, or share a glance
with me; show me your bracelet, hypnotise
us with the gleam of it. The purple glass
still glitters on your wrist. I want to dance
the way you can. I want to have the chance.

II.

We kissed, just once. The pair of us were drunk
(that is, you woke hung-over). You were dusk,
all skin, closed eyes, dark dress, the scent of musk
in well-breathed air: the sense of something sunk
next morning. Nothing happened. Nothing changed
between me and your smile. I think I knew
my courage had just given up on you —
the empty streets were filled with something strange

and lonely. It's not you, love. You were not
the answer, but a symbol. I still feel
sometimes, your arms around me — solid, real,
and not unkind — and there's a well-loved spot
of hot-pink memory, turned soft and mist:
a chance not taken, never second-kissed.

III.

We're scattering like dandelion seeds,
down-winged on darting winds, blowing in clouds
of dissipating fluff-silk parachutes:
the subtext isn't all that hard to read.
I won't see you again. You're blowing south
I think (I hope. Hot weather's right. It suits
the cream and scarlet of you.) Chances breed
in strange ways: you, you stood out in a crowd
and focused photographs. You hit REBOOT
on slow electrics. Thank you. I don't need
to say much, and the words don't fit my mouth:
"You're wild, you're lovely, strange, exciting, cute —"

just doesn't cover it. But I can try:
you're beautiful. Live fierce. Live well. Goodbye.

JACK UNDERWOOD

◊ ◊ ◊

Jack Underwood was born in Norwich in 1984. He graduated from Norwich School of Art and Design in 2005 and is currently completing a PhD in Creative Writing at Goldsmiths College, where he also teaches English Literature and Creative Writing. He is a librettist, musician and co-edits the anthology series *Stop Sharpening Your Knives*. He won an Eric Gregory Award in 2007 and was named a Faber New Poet in 2009. His debut pamphlet was published by Faber in October 2009 and his poems also feature in *Voice Recognition* from Bloodaxe. He reviews for *Ambit* and *Poetry London*. He lives in Hackney.

AND WHAT DO YOU DO?

Write codenames, military mainly.
"Operation blunt-tongue" that was me,
"spirit-hat", "yard-mile" them too.

I'm jacking it in next month:
civvy street, open shirt, slip on shoes.
I've a job lined-up in colours.

How about "burnt viscose", "black jam"?
Would you paint your hall with "easy money"?
These days there's little left to call.

What beautiful blue eyes you have.

UNDER

I was picking an apple when it spoke
in worm tongue: *youth is busy in you* it said
and sure enough my skin greened, a seed pip
lodged itself in each chamber of my pink heart.

Then while turning radishes, one pepper root
buzzed, a moth in my fist: *love will redden the veins,*
and whiten the fluids I felt it say. *Go home.*
Wash your hands, for girls cannot be dug at.

I walked the back-lanes where cow parsley dipped
and posed. One sprig I took and held to my nose,
giggled: *I am fed on the dead men of your house.*
There is fog inside you and I tasted my name.

Lover, if I am foggish and truly dying, if love
fleshes itself wordily and I am young enough to say,
if blood has taken root and swelled me to a man,
take me home, wash my hands.

MY OTHER GIRLFRIENDS

are all beautiful.
Eating figs with one of them or another
on holiday, it's as if the sky settles in,
the ground leans to stretch me out

201

and the sweet breeze dizzy with bugs
conspires for me to lift their skirts.

And when we step out in various towns,
jukeboxes singing from bars, a lager-top
fizzing, brightly earning condensation,
my other girlfriends multiply,
endlessly, beyond the wheel of the city
into swarms of swarms of girlfriends,
so that nothing in the world is not love
or how it tips our lives up
and I want to see the freckles
that are the enemy of dying
on the shoulder of my girlfriend
and only for her to be true.

CONSEQUENCES

I need to tell you that your elbow
fits fully in the nook under my chin,
that I want to put your lovely ear
up to my mouth and sing myself inside.

I'm so used to looking into your eyes,
I forget the names of colours.
I want to bend your knees. Your feet
are extremely well proportioned.

Now say "Avocado" and let me see
your armpit. I am a buffoon for you;
scratch my bright, scabby head.
Lace your shoes as usual.

CERTAIN

Nothing before had seemed so potent
and self-contained—
surely the onion was beautiful.

Its hung cloud of acid worked
in his nose and throat
as the knife bisected

like a maker of names passing
between twins, calling one half *Perfect*
the other also *Perfect*.

AHREN WARNER

◇ ◇ ◇

Ahren Warner was born in Oxford in 1986. His first collection *Confer* was published by Bloodaxe in 2011, while a pocket book, *Re:*, was published by Donut Press in early 2011. His work has been included in the anthologies *Identity Parade: New British and Irish Poets* (Bloodaxe, 2010), *Voice Recognition: 21 Poets for the 21st Century* (Bloodaxe, 2009) and *City State: New London Poetry* (Penned in the Margins, 2009).

JARDIN DU LUXEMBOURG

Here, all parks are masculine, grammatically so
I mean: *le jardin, le parc*, never a *la*.
Planes defined by avenues, circulars,
lines on the maps labelled with saints, saintly
politicos: Saint Michel, Kennedy, Jacques.

Even the flowers, here, are masculine;
reminding us of the season, a year or so back,
Gucci, or some such, had men preening
in powder-pink shirts, strutting their cocks
down the Strand, Bishopsgate, Bank.

Here, there are no pink shirts, hardly any
shirts at all. Just men, reclining in the bronze
of their *estomacs*; the vague swell of their guts
rising to the heat. There are women too, of course,
mostly with tops, but tops rolled up,

estomacs bared to the sun. We are reclining too,
squinting at the sky—as electric, if lighter
than Klein's—swallowed up or slipping in
to an igloo of *sérénité*, the gender of which
I've had neither the time, nor desire, to look up.

PICTOGRAMME

O, you—a hundred years from now—do you remember
the TV? It was shite really, a feckless invention;

nowhere near as useful as your gamma ray
carving knives, which both cook and cut together.

Either way, it was on TV that I heard
Senhora Rego declared "the greatest living painter

of woman's experience" by this bloke from Australia
(do you still have Australia, or have you

abolished it?). And, perhaps this is a moot point
for you, my highly evolved future readers,

but I wondered how he knew. I mean, how he
could know the *adequatio* of colour, line and texture

to the experience of something so utterly Other.
Here I'm speaking to you, future males; females

transpose the gender. On Avenue de l'Opéra
or Rue des Petits Champs, I find myself so often

fixated by a girl's *derrière*, trying to think over
the rubbing of two thighs; nothing between but air.

ENGRAM

As the wrinkled skin of milk over-boiled
conjures the sludge of moistening bath balls,

the pucker of wet paper—graphite's aquaplane—
summons up bubble bath, its faux clementine.

And, though I know that a single memory
so often beacons through our infant clutter

I'm surprised that (though only a decade ago)
I remember the red, the nap of the pyjamas

I shed for the bath; how urgent it seemed
to run bare-arsed and dangling

in search of a pen and the paper I'd hold
in muculent hands; each letter bleeding

to a smutch or shadow. I remember this.
I cannot remember my first kiss's name.

AVIS

Give them time to miss you   and if they don't
call   imagine that they want to   somewhere;

that their smile is there   but worn as cant
that whoever they're with   is a Gaussian blur

as are the trees   the redbreasts   the children
playing in the background   as they stare

beyond the scent   brimming in the kitchen
the tender fit   of another's hand

that gaggle of friends   laughing around them.
Think of their eyes   set on a point beyond

the earth's curve   or that stretch of summer
light   they wear like a cosy   burden

waiting   as they must be   for you.   Venture
hope;   that they might be happy   even there.

EPISTLE

Years away   or less   you do not know this song;
the way we drink to it   the stupefaction

of our dance   this girl who makes the air
gelatinous.   Your metaphors have changed;

your gut no longer turns   with her absence.
And no   our melodies are no more wedded

to the Phrygian   than are our hands content
kept clean of transgression.   Beyond this revelry

—these riffs   that seem to hold the sun   in solstice —
I   at least   am hopeless.   Beware the academics

who have read of us   and   might try to piece together
our revival   you'll find no masterworks

amongst our debris   this is not Pompeii
nor Ercolano   there are no signs of our times.

BEN WILKINSON

◇ ◇ ◇

Ben Wilkinson was born in Stafford, Staffordshire in 1985. He read English and Philosophy at the University of Sheffield, and was awarded an MA in Writing from Sheffield Hallam University. His pamphlet of poems, *The Sparks*, was published as part of tall-lighthouse's Pilot series. He regularly reviews new poetry for the *Guardian* and the *Times Literary Supplement*, and he was shortlisted for the 2010 Picador Poetry Prize. He lives and works in Sheffield, South Yorkshire.

FIRST GLANCE

Like *that*, the sudden hell-bent flap
of a pigeon at the window —
as if livid, bothered

by my lifting some slim volume
from a shelf,
rather than half-trapped,

taking glass for air
and flailing against a trick
of the light as much as itself,

reminds me of that time I saw
what I thought was you
(before I truly knew you)

kissing someone else,
only to find you, minutes later,
strolling up the street I was traipsing down.

FILTER

Out from the quay, and the trawler heading away to foreign waters
wobbles as if an apple bobbing in the kitchen basin of All Hallows' Eve.

Its dragnet of dregs, settling on the sea's black-misted base
of low-lying cod, haddock, the monstrous sub of the deep Atlantic salmon,

almost looks to be catching the water's beady-eyed contents
as if to expel its forty one million square miles of swallowing depression.

Returning, with so much fresh fish for tomorrow's hungry morning,
and the bulk of boat slow-shifts from foot to foot, tethered down to its
cobblestone jetty.

And yet, through some fathomless way of sunless ferment, next day
sees the sea ten strong or more, as if the trawler had never flounced

its many tons, shook its shivering skin above, the freezing depths
rippling beneath. The way the ocean filters up its once salt-ridden waters

to the streams and brooks inland, or how the Egyptian cobra shed its skin,
intact, carefully rubbing its head, leaving behind a perfect replica of itself.

SUNDAY

The rain lashing down like a TV's static
as smokers huddle under pubs' lintels—
from the Lescar across to Porter Cottage
the storm turns from drizzle to dismal.
Bless he who, with the cool persistence
of a craftsman, re-rolls a soggy Rizla,
opening the botched attempt in silence
as he rolls it into another.

When I leave with Jes, the sky has cleared:
a van trundles down Sharrowvale past
the shell of a butcher's, boarded and barred;
the sun and bulky nimbus in weird contrast
as I open up the Marlboros, offer her one,
struggling to recall if it was accident or arson.

THE RIVER DON

rushes by, a sudden current pushing on
past rows of fig trees blooming from its banks
and factories' warm outfalls, spilling nearby.
Remember how the floods two years back
rose to the mark etched on The Fat Cat's wall;
that third summer of ours when the rain did
nothing but pour, and the thought of what we
might wake to was the dream I'd been suffering
on/off for weeks?
                    It never reached us. We didn't
climb downstairs, half-asleep, to find our furniture
floating or ornaments, CDs and old cassette tapes
making their bids to escape. Instead, the house
sat safe and sound—floors dry, photo frames still,
something else edging closer, the way that water will.

SOPHIE YEO

◇　◇　◇

Sophie Yeo was born in Cardiff in 1989 and lives there still. She graduated in 2011 from the University of Oxford, where she studied English. She was commended in the Foyles Young Poet Competition in 2005 and 2006.

LOVE'S PROGRESS

Ceremonially, Love finds her place at the celebration table
and sucks a cherry, with the flick of a sycamore leaf over her eye
as if to say, I've travelled to the corners and crescents
of the earth in nature's own gilded vein, yet still
I dine with you,
my disciples.
Her skin softens into foie gras
and her hair naturally blows in the helicopter wind
of her own centuries of honourable flights.
She will dine with you, but you will drink more.
You know you will never quite get it right,
never quite know how to follow, when to laugh.
Love is slightly weary from the train,
the dust on her sleeve as grey as your restraint.

POEM

Every night a new monarch, it seemed.
With every ruler the kingdom changed.
Your mother was absurd to tell us
time wasn't as we'd have it, as she rode out each dawn
to the call of processional horns.

Time *was* as we'd have it,
always changing as we changed.
When he collected his cap from the branch,
Genesis was breeding on the new-sprung oak.
May Morning followed the birthday
we'd never shared till now, twinned
by the sudden expansion of one long blurred year
into yardsticks of weaning, schooling, and hiding.

We awoke to find primroses winking under thawing frost.
The petals were as light as charms and rustled in the breeze;
the frost wasted its blue in drawing our blood to the skin.
Only now its written do I think of paper and ink.
These are merely shadows scribed into exiled shapes.
I cannot presume to write the truth.

He watched me aging from afar
into the colour of charring corn,
for I was golden and roughed the fields
before he turned me black with rage.
The season's first rainfall left pools of our playing
brimful in the mill, to jump in, drench up,
when from the wisest tree the acorns came pouring.

Sunday never absolved us, but we didn't mind our sins
when we heard the bells tolling the time to sleep in.

CHRISTMAS, 1914

"Poor little God of love, born tonight, how can you love mankind?"

War diary, Lieutenant Maurice Laurentin

From the genesis in the trenches of a shattered God,
from the retraction of a gunshot in the convalescent man,
from the unity of raw herds of trained animals,
I was born. I rose from the churned lawn like clean vapour,
like a herb in the gassy hell of mud and blanched faces.

In such bare solitude, I created more than just a handshake.
I was a fume to wrap weak men in the metal arms
of each other, a frontier beyond the segregation of an army.
I ascended, a fertilized deity, bringing a fir tree.

Who does not love their flawed creations for their gift
of identity? Oranges and tobacco replaced the bodies;
the fragile sound of hymns from a glass harmonica
overrode the thorny echoes of gunshots. How could I not
love the naivety of such impromptu and natural forgiveness?

I was born from the womb of a mother who, for the loss
of a heartbeat, had not forgotten about the inside need
yet for life; and I am asked how I can love mankind?

NOCTURNE

I.

The small urban worlds seemed so certain
that even we, with our studious expressions,
knew we could never dismiss such a form of art:
here were scribbles becoming geometry.

At the focus of the twenty centimetre canvas,
the sky and the pavement became cross linked.
Cones, crescent moons and satellites were etched
with such logic and austerity that we were charmed
from the idea that all paintings gleamed with sentiment.

I analysed in a cool but passionate tone,
realising the restraints of angles and semi-circles
while you made analogies to real life, keeping your eyes
stuck steady to the wall, unable to meet mine.
"That octagon, you." "Those parallel lines, us."

I told you, on a whim, that I would measure
each angle that the artist had drawn to create us
a new dimension from their sum. You agreed
to stand by me if I did; you'd had the same thought.

Those parallel lines, no matter how far they run . . .

II.

My lane was silent but for the shuffling in of jaded weather.
How could I have moved my hands with your fingers
laid bare on my eyes? I always turned my back
to the piano as I played, afraid of your face robed in the music.
The faithless silence was the homecoming for your thoughts:

your mind withdrew from the dangerous steps we'd made together
from classicism to impressionism. Any resonance of former sound
would have tempted your mind with our old reflections,
and your concern was with the letter received at seven that morning.

Your mother was craving flowers. She was back to the beginning.
I watched your eyes scroll down the page again and again
from the swing in my back garden. I wanted to help.

When it came to plants, I knew all the names in Latin.
With the page folded like felt, scratching at your heart, in your
chest pocket, you read the labels on my potted plants, and then on
you went riding. The disbelief that you had seen my house
oblivious to the single squeak of its swing where once there were two
sent the acrobats in my head in heavy somersaults to my feet.

III.

Nocturnal events fall in time with love, and that is something
that can only happen unexpectedly, darker from the impact.
It was a time when the night was star-cold, the stars sky-clawed.
Pond life and crickets seethed into shapes on astronomers' maps
among the reeds. The fairground galloped to town with wagons and whips,
and suspended ropes emerged, bizarre and shimmering, from the still-born
   world.

I felt the grass beneath my feet like a million tightropes,
no longer grey and serene but dew in contradistinction
to moonlight, twitching, frantic and glittering like iron filings.
The risk was wanting you with me amid the undeniable romance
of an evening so alive with oscillations and onion-bleached lights,
gypsy wedding dresses and dances in the bandstand!
On the way, you spiralled and laughed to the music in the pipes
of the caravans, while I listened out for dissonance.

IV.

Your peace turned turbulent, and a carousel of forlorn
prayer hung in the air like unwanted pearls, fluid sapphire
with the screams of a boy who was wrecked by a stranger.
As you receded to your attic in isolation, you finally decided
that the Roman candles twinkling in the lake and overlooked
by lovers must be vandalism. You miscreated, I miscalculated.

Things fall apart and nothing is certain. You fell apart.
If you found my life false, then should truth have mattered?
You gasped pain and names into the patchwork blanket
stitched by your mother in childhood, now faded with neglect.
The querulous twilight was white and dry, flaking silver
into the street that would be gone by morning.

You never told anyone if you lived or died.
Into the night fell promises that no one remembered making.

ACKNOWLEDGEMENTS

Dan Barrow: "An Inheritance" was first published at *Horizon Review*. "2nd June 1916" was first published at *The Cadaverine*.

Jack Belloli: "Loquation" is a revised version of "Tendencies to Shape', published in *Intimate Distances* (Christ's College Cambridge, 2010).

Jay Bernard: "Tuesday Morning" and "Migration" first appeared in *Your Sign is Cuckoo, Girl* (tall-lighthouse).

Penny Boxall: "Navigavi" was highly commended in the 2010 Museum of London poetry competition. "Williams, Who Lived" came third in the Segora poetry competition, 2010.

James Brookes: "Opiates: Kalingrad" was first published in *The Wolf*, "Hierophantic Head of Mao, Hunan Province" in *The Rialto*, "In Clitheroe Keep I" in *Horizon Review*. "In Clitheroe Keep I" and "The English Sweats" were in the pamphlet *The English Sweats* (Pighog Press, 2009).

Phil Brown: "Diptych" was first published in *Magma*. "Sir Gawain on the Northern Line" was first published in *Dove Release: New Flights and Voices* (Worple, 2010).

Niall Campbell: "Hitching Lifts from Islanders" and "Interrupting Boccaccio" were first published in Blackbox Manifold and Cyphers, respectfully.

Kayo Chingonyi: "Gnosis" was first published at *Pomegranate*, "Fist of the North Star" appeared at *Mercy E-zine* and "Some Bright Elegance" is featured on *Poetry International Web*.

John Clegg: "Antler" and "Moss" were in the e-chapbook *Advancer* (Silkworms Ink, 2010). "Kayaks" was first published in *Horizon Review*. "Tribe" was first published in *Succour*.

Amy De'Ath: "Sonnet" and "Poetry for Boys" were first published in *Erec & Enide* (Salt, 2010).

Inua Ellams: "GuerrillaGardenWritingPoem" was first published in the anthology *City State* (*Penned in the Margins*, 2009) and in *Untitled*.

Charlotte Geater: "Moro" was first published in *The Mays XVII*. "Grotesquerie" was first published in The Rialto.

Dai George: "New Translation" was first published in *The Boston Review*.

Tom Gilliver: "Talking Back" and "Before We Thaw" were first published in *Poetry Review*.

Emily Hasler: "Cake Fork" appears in *Clinic 2*. "Wet Season" was awarded second prize in the 2009 Edwin Morgan International Poetry Competition. "The Cormorants" was included in the anthology *Dove Release: New Flights and Voices* (Worple Press 2010) with the title of "Cormorant'. "On reading the meaning of "falchion" in an encyclopaedia" was first published in *Warwick Review*.

Oli Hazzard: "Moving In', "Arrival" and "Badlands" were first published in *PN Review*. "Prelude to Growth" was first published in *Clinic*. "The Inability To Recall The Precise Word For Something" appeared in *Poetry Salzburg Review*.

Daniel Hitchens: "Fruitbowl" was first published in *Magma*. Election 2010: A Poetic Review appeared in full in *Pomegranate*.

Sarah Howe: "Faults Escaped" appeared in *A Certain Chinese Encyclopdeia* (tall-lighthouse).

Andrew Jamison: "The Bus from Belfast" was first published in *The Rialto*. "The Starlings" was first published in *The Ulster Tatler*. "Death's Door" was first published in *The Yellow Nib*.

Annie Katchinska: " Blue'," February" and" Toni Braxton" were published in *Faber New Poets 6*.
"Toni Braxton" was published in *Voice Recognition* (Bloodaxe).

Andrew McMillan: "Nabokov's butterflies" was first published in *Horizon Review*. "6:30am" was in the pamphlet *every salt advance* (Red Squirrel Press, 2009). "obituary of a lesser East-European poet" was first published in *Prole*. "in my dreams you walk dripping from a sea journey on the highway across America" takes its name from a line in Ginsberg's Howl.

Siofra McSherry: "Sleepless" was first published as "Insomnia" in foam:e.

Ben Maier: "A Short History of Textiles" was first published at From the Fishouse (www.fishousepoems.org).

Laura Marsh: Apollo's Hyacinths was first published at Pomegranate.

Annabella Massey: "Istanbul" was first published in INK.

James Midgley: "Butterfly Antennae" was commissioned by TATE ETC. and published online as their poem of the month. "The Invention of Faces" was first published in The Rialto.

Helen Mort: "A Chaser for Miss Heath" was first published in the pamphlet A Pint for the Ghost, (tall-lighthouse, 2010)

Richard O'Brien: "Moses in Medieval Glass" was in the pamphlet your own devices (tall-lighthouse press, 2009)

Richard Osmond: "Anatomist" first appeared in the mays xviii (Varsity Publications, 2010).

Vidyan Ravinthiran "Ma" was first published in Smiths Knoll; "Jump-cuts', "Recession" and "Dot Dot Dot" appeared in Iota.

Sophie Robinson: "Flesh Leggings" and "Winded by Love" have been published in The Lotion (Old Hunstanton: Oystercatcher, 2010)

Charlotte Runcie: "The Seventh Winter', "Pope, Telescope" and "Fur" appeared in Seventeen Horse Skeletons (tall-lighthouse). "In My Pocket" was in Coin Opera 2 (Sidekick Books).

Colette Sensier: "Toothlessness" was first published at nthposition. "Orpheus" was first published in Iota. "Evolution" was first published at Cadaverine and has also been published at Mercy.

Lavinia Singer: "The Mapmaker's Daughter" was published in Poetry Review.

Adham Smart: An older version of "The New Mechanics" was first recorded for the *Poetry Society Youth Members Magazine*. This version was commended in the *Seeing Further* Poems on the Underground competition 2010. "Pumpkin Heart Boy" was first published in *Eyewear*.

Emily Tesh: "Three Sonnets for a Girl" was first published in *Magma*.

Jack Underwood: "Certain" and "And what do you do?" were published in *Faber New Poets 4: Jack Underwood* in 2009. "Consequences" appears in *Stop Sharpening Your Knives 4*, and "Under" was published online at *The Best American Poetry*.

Ahren Warner: "Jardin du Luxembourg" and "Epistle" appeared previously in a pocket book, *Re:* (Donut Press, 2011). "Epistle" also appeared in the anthology *Voice Recognition: 21 Poets for the 21st Century* (Bloodaxe Books, 2009)

Ben Wilkinson: "First Glance" was first published in the *Times Literary Supplement*. "Filter" first appeared in *Poetry Review*, and subsequently in *The Sparks* (tall-lighthouse, 2008). "Sunday" first appeared in *Poetry London*, and subsequently in *The Sparks*. "The River Don" was first published in *The Spectator*.

Sophie Yeo: "Love's Progress" and "Nocturne" both appeared at *PoetCasting*.

JUN 0 6 2016 **DATE DUE**

CPSIA information can be obtained at www.ICGtesting.com
Printed in the USA
BVOW05s1939220516

449115BV00004B/102/P

9 781907 773105